This book will encourage the heart
and women who serve in the Armed
fire—desperately needed in this hour in America—for patriotism.

—REVEREND RALEIGH B. WASHINGTON, DD; Lt. Col. US Army (Ret); recipient of the Bronze Star for Meritorious Service in Vietnam; president and chief executive officer, Promise Keepers

Charlene captures the indomitable spirit of courage, faith, duty, and commitment. Her dad's story highlights that the experiences of WWII not only created heroes but produced Americans with impeccable character. I highly recommend this book; it will be difficult to put it down.

—WILLIAM O. WASHINGTON, PhD, senior vice president for student affairs, dean of students (college), chair of student leadership, Trinity International University

Five stars. This is an extraordinary book by a magnificent writer. Charlene Quint Kalebic's captivating charm is coupled with a brilliance that sets her apart even from the cadre of exceptional writers. *The Angels of Ebermannstadt* is a special love story that every soldier, from the Greatest Generation to those currently serving, will want to experience. As the years pass by, all of us would like to be seventeen again. You can be and you will be as you read this captivating story.

—ORLEY R. HERRON, PhD, Lt. Cmdr. US Navy (Ret); Navy Chaplain (Ret); former president, National Louis University; former president, Greenville College

Angels of Ebermannstadt is a lovely tribute to the Greatest Generation, but more specifically, to the endearing wartime acts of kindness by average American soldiers, many of whom were still in their teens. It is a many-faceted and uplifting story of good over evil and of how the human spirit somehow triumphs in the face of the carnage and inhumanity wrought by war. It also shines light on the terrible suffering by non-combatants on both sides of the battlefield. The author has, in essence, written a love story—love of country, love of parents, and love for all of God's children. Hopefully Charlene's journey back in time will remind future generations of "those who gave their todays for our tomorrows."

—JOHN W. BITOFF, Rear Admiral, US Navy (Ret), member, board of directors, Friends of the National World War II Memorial

Experiencing history as it unfolds from a very personal point of view is part of our collective treasure that needs to be memorialized for future generations. *Angels of Ebermannstadt* offers context to why we call it "The Greatest Generation"!

—TOMMY L. DAVIS, former CEO, Indecon, Inc.; presidential associate, Galen Center; founder, Zemeckis Center, University of Southern California

ANGELS
of EBERMANNSTADT

The Journey of an Honored Soldier, a Daughter,
and Life's Greatest Lessons of Faith and Friendship

CHARLENE QUINT KALEBIC

All Scripture quotations, unless otherwise indicated, are taken from the Holy Bible,
New International Version®. NIV®. Copyright © 1973, 1978, 1984 by International
Bible Society. Used by permission of Zondervan. All rights reserved.

Scripture marked "KJV" is taken from the King James Version of the Holy Bible.
Public domain.

Published by
Deep River Books
Sisters, Oregon
www.deepriverbooks.com

ISBN-10: 1937756475
ISBN-13: 9781937756475

Library of Congress: 9781937756475
Printed in the USA

Design by Robin Black, www.blackbirdcreative.biz

CONTENTS

Dedicated to the brave men and women of the armed services who have courageously served our country and, in so doing, have fanned the flames of liberty at home and abroad. A grateful nation thanks you. We are forever in your debt.

With love to my family: you have been my greatest joy and have made me a better person.

With special thanks to Orley R. Herron for your encouragement and friendship.

In loving memory of my dad, Dick Quint, my greatest teacher, and in honor of my mom, Jean, the love of his life.

With love and friendship to the Angels of Ebermannstadt.

With humble thanks to God for all the good gifts He has bestowed.

In grateful appreciation of the men and women who have served our country, a portion of the proceeds of the sale of this book will be given to charities which assist wounded veterans.

FOREWORD

The Fourth Commandment exhorts all of us to honor our fathers and mothers. Charlene Quint Kalebic fulfills that commandment elegantly with this book, which honors her father's return journey to the battlefields he traversed in World War II. She takes us back to the year her father enlisted at the young age of seventeen. Right from the start, we are drawn into this journey, not as observers, but as fellow travelers, there beside her father as he revisits those hallowed grounds anointed by the blood of so many.

Angels of Ebermannstadt is a special love story—a story of faith in the midst of the horrors of war, lifelong friendships regardless of nationality, and passing to the next generation life's most important lessons.

From those of us who have worn the uniform of service—thank you, Charlene, for transporting us back to our youth, to recall again our fears and hopes as we prayed for courage and safekeeping while in harm's way.

God bless America, and God bless those who defend her. God bless our noble Richard Quint and God bless his daughter, Charlene Quint Kalebic.

Orley R. Herron, PhD
Lt. Cmdr. US Navy, Retired
Navy Chaplain, Retired
Former President, National Louis University
Former President, Greenville College

THE OCTOGENARIANS

The Octogenarians—
They are a bit slower than the rest of us.
They have run their race—and they have won.
They have heard the words "Well done, my good and faithful servant."
They are now walking their victory lap.

The Octogenarians—
They are a bit more thankful than the rest of us.
They have endured the Depression with hole-ridden shoes
and hungry stomachs.
They have survived a war—crawling on their bellies with
the blood of a fallen soldier and friend
splattered on their fatigues.
They have witnessed injustice—and were compelled to right a wrong.
Yet their hearts have been moved by the kindness of strangers,
the warmth of friendship, the love of family.
They have seen the worst mankind has to offer—and the best.
And still, they are thankful.
They have no time to dwell on that which has not been given,
they are much too occupied being thankful for that which has.

The Octogenarians—
Their love of their country is a bit stronger than the rest of ours.
Their commitment runs deep within their souls.
They are as much a part of America as America is a part of them.
When war called—they answered,
Knowing, as their forefathers before them,
that the liberty this country offers
can only be purchased with the precious blood
of those willing to die for freedom.

The Octogenarians—
They are a bit more content than the rest of us.
Their serenity shows in the twinkle of their eyes and
in the peace on their countenances.
They have been in the midst of wealth;
they have seen unthinkable poverty.
Yet they have found the secret to contentment in every situation.

The Octogenarians—
They are a bit wiser than the rest of us.
Years of experience have given them insight into the human soul.
They know that the fear of the Lord is the first step toward wisdom.
And they have reaped the blessings of a life lived with
wisdom and grace and righteousness.

The Octogenarians—
They are a bit more like God than the rest of us.
Just like children, so fresh from the hand of God, are Godlike,
So too are the octogenarians, as our Lord draws them
closer to home—and to Him.

The Octogenarians—
Are they a bit more blessed than the rest of us?
I think not.
For it is I who am blessed
Because I was chosen to be their child.
For it is I who am blessed
Because I am a part of them.
For it is I who am blessed
Because they are in me.

CHARLENE Q. KALEBIC

"When you are kind to others,
it not only changes you,
it changes the world."

—HAROLD KUSHNER

INTRODUCTION

It wasn't until I hit forty that I realized my life was already half-lived, and more importantly, that my parents, both in their eighties, would not be around forever. All of those things on my to-do list, everything I was going to get around to someday, I needed to get around to sooner rather than later because there might not be any later. And one of those things I felt compelled to do as I got older was to get to know more about my dad in the younger years of his life.

My father, Richard Quint, had been an infantryman in World War II—"The Big One," as he called it. But like almost everyone from his generation, he never talked about it. He never talked about the war, or what he saw, or how he got his medals. Mother said that even into the 1960s, he would have nightmares about the war and wake up screaming, but he never talked about it to her either. Occasionally I would hear a snippet here or there about a family he'd stayed with or a person he might have met or his horse when he was in the horse-drawn field artillery. But generally, that part of his history was a big black hole.

If you know my dad, you know that for him, not talking about something is next to impossible. I've never met a person who didn't like him or call him friend, and I've never heard him say an unkind word about anyone (with the possible exception of his first wife). No matter whom he met, whether it was a farmer or a secretary or a businessman, he would find something in common and the conversation would flow like sweet tea on a hot day.

A machinist and tool-and-die maker by trade, with a garage full of "treasures" like lathes and drill presses and every other mechanical tool dreamed up by the mind of man, he spent most of his time puttering about town helping out anyone who needed a hand: "I've got to fix the back door for Mrs. French" or "I'm going out to the Gweynn's farm to help with their tractor" or "Gotta head out to the shop to make a tool for Bob's machine that locked up last week." At gun club meetings, tractor pulls, Ducks Unlimited gatherings, American Legion get-togethers, or farm auctions, he could talk to someone he knew for hours, and a stranger even longer. Somewhere in the conversation, Dad would say something like, "Oh, I have just the thing you are looking for!" And they would exchange phone numbers, set up a time to work on a project, and pretty soon Dad had a new friend. It drove Mother crazy. She did not see the point of wasting time making new friends. With his old manual typewriter and his rotary telephone, he kept in touch with more people around the world than I could possibly find in my Rolodex. So his complete silence on the subject of World War II was absolutely out of character, and I decided I needed to know more about it. After all, those were his formative years—he enlisted at the age of seventeen—and there must have been something lurking there that made him the person he was today.

The sixtieth anniversary of the Allied invasion of June 6, 1944 provided the perfect opportunity to get to know more about those unknown years. In the fall of 2003, almost on a lark, I called and asked if he would want to go to Europe for the sixtieth. I suggested that we could retrace his footsteps from World War II and that he could be our tour guide. It took him all of a nanosecond to say yes. The very next day he faxed what he considered to be the ideal itinerary, which included no less than eighteen cities in five different countries. I giggled when I received it—Dad's sense of adventure always outweighed our allotment of time. I cut it down to what we could reasonably expect to accomplish in a two-week vacation and started making plans.

Leaving behind my son Donny (then seventeen) to finish high school finals in the company of my mother, who was no more interested in all this "unnecessary fall-de-rah" as she called it than Donny was, in May of 2004 my husband, Tom, our two youngest children, nine-year-old Christy and five-year-old Marty, Dad, and I embarked upon our historical expedition to retrace the footsteps of a soldier as he had landed on Omaha Beach and marched to Berlin. Although I considered myself educated and fairly well-read (after all, I had a law degree and managed to read a fair amount at least in the areas of law and business), I was completely unprepared for the amazing education the simple people in our party and those we would meet on our trip would teach us. Little did we know this trip would grip our hearts, enlighten our minds, teach us lessons in international relations, and forever change the way we viewed the world and "the Greatest Generation."

RETRACING THE FOOTSTEPS
Our Great Adventure with the Greatest Generation

SATURDAY, MAY 29, 2004, LAKE FOREST, ILLINOIS
*"Greater love has no man than this,
that he lay down his life for his friends."*
—JOHN 15:12

After lying in bed and thinking about the days to come, I finally crawled out at seven a.m. Tom was already awake. I padded softly downstairs to the smell of fresh coffee and grabbed a cup. At least coffee was on my clear-liquids-only diet—doctor's orders. I was just released from the hospital last night after a painful bout of diverticulitis. When I went in to the hospital (by way of the emergency room) on Thursday, the attending physician attempted to tell me that I would be in for several more days when I interrupted and told him, matter-of-factly, that I would be leaving on an airplane on Saturday to take my father to the sixtieth anniversary of D-Day, and that whatever he needed to do to make sure I was on that plane, he should do it. He kept me in the hospital another day and sent me home with a handful of drugs and strict instructions to stick to a diet of clear liquids—which unfortunately does *not* include German beer.

As I looked out the window, the rain started to softly pour, and I thought of the days before June 6, 1944—rainy, stormy, cold. *What must it have felt like to be a GI getting ready to invade Normandy? What were they thinking and feeling? Excitement? Ready for a fight? Sick to their stomachs? Scared? Sheer terror? All of the above?* I wondered if any of them felt as sick as I have been these last two days. I'm sure some were. I'm sure they fought anyway.

I think of the war we are now in to free the Iraqis. *Will they ever learn how to govern themselves? I don't know, but so far, I think not,* was my reply to myself.

What makes America so great? I wondered, as I have wondered many times, especially since the beginning of the Second Gulf War. Today the question is prompted by my reflections over the events of the past weeks and months. Although I don't normally cry when I read the *Wall Street Journal*—after all, it's a business newspaper—I cried when I read it last Tuesday. The story of a young corporal who had reenlisted, even though his tour of duty was over in July, to make sure his company all made it home safe and to make sure his buddy could see his wife again, had brought tears to my eyes. When a grenade thrown from an Iraqi's hand was about to explode, Corporal Jason L. Dunham dove and covered the grenade with his helmet and his body to save the marines around him. He never made it home, but his company did, thanks to him.[1]

This morning, the answer finally revealed itself to me, as it had revealed itself to Alexis de Tocqueville some 170 years before: *America's greatness is because of its goodness.* A fanatical Muslim will sacrifice himself (with a suicide bomb attached) to kill others out of hatred. But an American marine will sacrifice himself (and throw himself on a grenade) to save others—his buddies and his family—out of love. And therein lies the whole difference.

---

1   Corporal Jason L. Dunham posthumously received the Congressional
    Medal of Honor, America's highest military award, on November 10,
    2006, what would have been his twenty-fifth birthday.

Today we embark on a trip to remember America's goodness. We go to remember those brave soldiers who crossed the English Channel in unthinkable weather to face unimaginable brutality and hatred—in short, to save Europe and the rest of the world from the barbaric Nazis. They changed the course of history. They were scared, but they went anyway. And that, I suppose, is the definition of bravery.

SUNDAY, MAY 30, 2004, ON A PLANE SOMEWHERE OVER THE ATLANTIC

The rest of yesterday went as smoothly as can be expected with present-day air travel. Airport electronic "self-serve" check-in never is, and we required the help of a service attendant for about half an hour. Even putting the bags through the X-ray machine proved comical as Dad and Tom hurried to save their precious camera film from disaster.

The most humorous part, as expected, was Dad going through the X-ray at security. I had warned Mother of this, as I know Dad loves to stash his pockets with grandpa-like things—notebooks, medicine, coins, a pocket knife, pens, etc. I suggested to her that he put these things in a carry-on bag and dump the pocket knife. The admonitions had obviously fallen on deaf ears (either hers or his) as Dad buzzed the walk-through security gate loaded with metal, including the metal rod in his leg—a little remembrance he had received after breaking his leg while falling from a ladder picking apples from his prized apple tree. One by one, Dad removed each little thing from a hidden pocket as the metal detector buzzed to point out some new violation. And to each offending item, whether a metal spiral on a notebook or the foil on the backside of a medicine packet, Dad responded with the same surprised answer: "Well, I didn't know *that* would set it off!"

After about the tenth occurrence, even the steely security guard was laughing. Marty, our five-year-old, was the only one who failed to be amused. He stood next to Grandpa the entire time with a furrowed brow, not at all seeing the humor in the situation and quite concerned that his beloved grandfather might never make it through.

I suppose sixty years ago, air travel to Europe was not quite such an issue or as complicated as the troops boarded. Every GI took all his belongings, including his gun *and* pocket knife, loaded on a cargo plane along with a few hundred others, and set out across the Atlantic to shoot and be shot at.

We finally made our way through the metal detectors at O'Hare and boarded our plane to Munich. Our family is not a shy one. Part of the fun of travel for everyone is meeting new people along the way. As we chatted with our male flight attendant and told him of our purpose for the flight, he said, "It's an honor to have your father with us." That was a pleasant surprise, and a nice start to our journey.

MONDAY MORNING, MAY 31, 2004, MUNICH

We landed at the Munich airport yesterday afternoon. I couldn't help but notice the airport's modern, clean, German style of glass and chrome. It was a masterpiece of engineering excellence. As I walked through its long corridors, I wondered what the German people thought of the sixtieth anniversary D-Day remembrances and the whole World War II era. *Do they welcome us? Do they see the Americans as their liberators? Or is there still some animosity? How do they view their past? Are they celebrating this anniversary—or dreading the remembrance of a brutal time in their history?* I decided that, despite my excitement, I should probably keep quiet about the purpose of our trip while I was in Germany.

Dad must have felt ill at ease as well. As soon as we stepped off the plane, he took off his favorite hat, complete with camouflage and military pins, and donned a nondescript baseball cap.

After dropping our luggage at our hotel and surveying our new home for the next few days, the first order of business was to find an outdoor *Brauhaus* in the center of town and settle down for some lunch and people-watching. The menu was quite limited by American standards—sausages, potatoes, and cheese. Marty was not at all convinced that the white sausage I told him was a hot dog was, in fact, a hot dog. We left a fair amount of lunch uneaten but managed to down all the ice cream. As my husband happily ate his sauerkraut, I recalled the story my dad had told about cabbages when I was a little girl, which he cheerfully retold as we were eating at the restaurant.

"I had always hated cooked cabbage until, at one point in the war, my company had gone for days without eating as we went through Belgium on our way toward Berlin. When we finally arrived in Germany, the only thing available from the mess tent was cooked cabbage. We devoured it like it was steak. And I've liked it ever since."

Thank goodness I had, quite by accident, discovered the perfect location for a hotel—within walking distance to the center of town and only a block from McDonald's (the favorite restaurant of our entire family with the exception of my husband, who prefers opposite extremes—either white tablecloths or White Castle). Having had enough of sausages, I snuck out for a Big Mac run late last night—to the delight of all.

Monday Evening, May 31, 2004, Munich
> *"If my people, who are called by my name, will humble themselves and pray and seek my face and turn from their wicked ways, then I will hear from heaven and forgive their sin and will heal their land."*
>
> —2 Chronicles 7:14

We began our exploration of Munich in earnest today. Tom and the kids took a bike tour led by a friendly, crazy Aussie at Mike's Bike Tours while Dad and I set off on our own. Dad wisely decided to take a test run on a bicycle before committing to the ride. As he explained to the tour guide, who graciously let him borrow his bike for the test run, he has not ridden a bicycle since 1947. This admission caused more than a few giggles among the twenty-something, dreadlock-laden, nose-ring-bearing tour guides. (When Dad inquired what was in his potential tour guide's eye, the eyebrow ring was the subject of a stilted and nervous laugh.)

Not quite sure that his eighty-two-year-old legs were up to a day-long bike ride, Dad and I opted for a rickshaw ride with an authentic, reserved, and piercing-free German. Being a history enthusiast (due to ignorance, not expertise), I requested the deluxe history tour. Johann, our guide who hailed from Salzburg, Austria, dutifully explained in grueling detail the history of Munich, from the monks who founded the town in the ninth century all the way through its many eccentric kings, as he pedaled through the backstreets and landmarks of the city. The history lesson, however, stopped abruptly at 1918, as if the last eighty years had not existed. Curiosity overcoming my better judgment, I gingerly asked when the era of the kings had ended and what forms of government they'd had since. He mentioned a few forms of governmental experiments in the "golden twenties" after the kings, and then mentioned the Nazis (almost as if in passing) in the thirties and forties. He never mentioned Hitler's name.

I finally had to ask—and our tour guide was the logical choice to ask it of. "How do the modern-day Germans deal with the history of the Nazis?"

There was a pregnant, uncomfortable pause. "Not very well," he explained. "They just don't know what to do or how to feel about such a horrible period where everyone in Germany seemed to have gone mad. Mostly, they just don't talk about it."

Feeling that I had asked as much as I politely could, I retreated to less sensitive questions, like how Germans viewed the move of the capital to Berlin. At first, he explained, the West Germans were resentful that hundreds of millions of euros were spent on new capitol buildings and infrastructure in Berlin, when the historic buildings here in Munich were perfectly suitable. They did not buy into the "unification-of-East-and-West-into-one-Germany" concept foisted upon them after the fall of the Berlin Wall. Apparently, people have gotten used to the idea, and it is now generally seen as a good thing.

After our tour, Dad and I stopped for coffee at McDonald's, one of our favorite activities to do together. I had brought my video camera for our historic trip in the hopes of making a documentary. So as we sipped our coffee in Micky D's, I interviewed Dad about his military service and first trip to Germany. After several minutes, all the activity and talking made him tired, and I walked him back to the hotel for a nap.

I spent the next few hours touring the king's palace. Again, the guided tours narrating the history of the buildings never mentioned the Third Reich, Hitler, or the Nazis.

How curious. Compared to America, where we self-examine and expose our every flaw in excruciating detail, from Christopher Columbus to slavery to present-day prison conditions in Iraq, the complete silence on the subject of the Nazis seems quite odd—as if repressing a bad memory. I'm not sure which is the best approach: apologizing for a country's every mistake or pretending they never happened. But it seems that at least some occasional self-reflection is the only way to learn from the past and progress. Ostriches don't seem to evolve very well.

I stopped at Mike's Tours to pick up our tickets for the following day's tour and chatted with Chris, the friendly twenty-something tour guide from New Jersey. After I explained the purpose of our trip (and after making sure there were no Germans within hearing distance), he wordlessly set out his hands and made a bowing motion, as if bowing to a king. I was a bit surprised at his reaction. He responded to my look of bewilderment, "For people of my generation, the men of World War II are men we don't know very many of; my contemporaries hold the World War II veterans in *huge* amounts of respect and a sense of awe."

Mmm. Another reality check for me, along with a perspective from the Gen Xers. It's strange how one can live with someone and think there is nothing special about that person while others hold them in "hero-worship" status.

The evening ended at the HofBrauhaus, a casual beer house, with more sausages and potatoes along with some mystery meat that was masquerading on the menu as meat loaf—but looking a whole lot like a sausage stuffed in a loaf pan. I concluded that the Germans could make sausage out of anything, even asparagus, if given the chance. I determined to make the best of it. With the oompah band clearly catering to this mostly American audience, the few Germans who were there looked at us with bewilderment as we belted out John Denver's "Take Me Home, Country Roads," only to be followed by an even louder rendition of "God Bless America."

I suppose it was then that I had another epiphany. *We were here singing "God Bless America" in a beer house, and the beautiful city of Munich was here with its variety of shops and culture, because my dad and hundreds of thousands like him came and fought for a free Europe. This entire country, as well as the rest of Europe, was the fruit of their labor.* The Germans had responded, it seems, with the appropriate response of someone who has been given a lifeline of salvation from what otherwise would have been a horrible demise: they set to work rebuilding their cities and improving themselves, excelling at what post-World War II Germans do best—engineering. And they repressed the whole terrible Nazi experience.

Perhaps our reaction to those times when we are given a second chance at life—whether recovering from a dreaded disease, narrowly escaping a horrible accident, or being rescued from our own path of self-destruction—should be that of the Germans: getting to the task of improving ourselves and paying forward the blessing by helping someone else. It has been said that God is a God of second chances. No matter what horrible things we may have done in our past, if we earnestly seek Him, He is ready to meet us wherever we are and bless us once again. And perhaps the people of Germany—home to the monks who founded Munich, Martin Luther, the Reformation, great cathedrals, millions of God-fearing people, . . . and Hitler—know this lesson better than any of us.

I don't know, but I suspect one reason the Germans were not enthusiastic about joining the United States in our action in Iraq was because they are quite aware that, in World War II, they invaded every country in their path. And now they do not want to be perceived in any way as repeating their mistakes by "invading" another country. Perhaps they are ashamed of their warmongering past and simply want nothing to do with being involved in starting another war. It's just my own theory, but I think a plausible one.

Tuesday Evening, June 1, 2004, Munich
"The folly of kings is their demise."
    —Charlene Quint Kalebic

With the exception of the children, none of us slept much last night. Tom had a cold, and I still heard him snoring when I looked over at the alarm clock at 4:09 a.m. But I couldn't sleep because my head was filled with the events of the day, like a movie on continuous rerun, and with the anticipation of retracing Dad's footsteps through Europe. I suspect that Dad's sleeplessness was due to the same reason, although he didn't share it with me.

A tired crew boarded the bus for a tour of Neuschwanstein, led by Tyrone, our friendly and irreverent tour guide from Cincinnati. Our plans for a tandem parasail from a nearby mountain quickly vanished as the weather turned to rain. Tom took a bike tour around Swan Lake with the rest of the tour, while the kids, Grandpa, and I took a gondola ride up the mountain for a breathtaking view of the castle and countryside. The kids seemed completely unimpressed with the view and were much more focused on watching the few paragliders who dared venture out in the rain.

The castle was magnificent, of course. Nestled in the Bavarian forest atop a rugged, evergreen-filled crag, with a backdrop of snowcapped Alps, the exterior beauty far surpassed anything I had seen in photographs. Once we were inside, each room was even more exquisite than the last. With its signature blue and gold furnishings and elegant swan theme, it was fit for, well, a king. However, only one-third of the rooms were ever completely decorated before King Ludwig died, even though he had been working on it for seventeen years or so.

I quickly realized that the reason for the slow interior-decorating process, which is time-consuming in even the best of circumstances, was that he'd had murals painted of a Wagnerian opera on each wall of every room. He must have kept all the artists in Bavaria employed for years! After falling victim to the souvenir shop at the end of the castle tour, we trekked the twenty-five-minute walk down the hill in the rain and boarded the bus back for Munich.

We couldn't bear to eat any more sausages, so we opted to dine at the little Italian restaurant recommended by Tyrone. We knew it must be good if approved by someone with Cincinnati taste buds. We weren't disappointed and finally satisfied a pizza and pasta craving.

WEDNESDAY EVENING, JUNE 2, 2004, A CUTE LITTLE HOUSE IN SCHLAIFHAUSEN, GERMANY

"In this life we cannot do great things. We can do only small things with great love."

—MOTHER TERESA

"[Jesus] said, 'I tell you the truth, unless you change and become like little children, you will never enter the kingdom of heaven. Therefore, whoever humbles himself like this child is the greatest in the kingdom of heaven. And whoever welcomes a little child like this in my name welcomes me. See that you do not look down on one of these little ones. For I tell you that their angels in heaven always see the face of my Father in heaven.'"

—MATTHEW 18:3–5, 10–11

Today was the highlight of our trip so far. We traveled by train to Nuremberg to meet dear friends of Dad's from World War II—his beloved Angels of Ebermannstadt. The history of their friendship needs some explaining. I have only heard it in bits and pieces, but when put all together, it goes something like this:

When Dad and the other American soldiers arrived in Germany, one of the tiny towns they liberated from the Nazis was Ebermannstadt, in Bavaria. While they were there, the Americans were kind to the townspeople. Dad, always the avid photographer, snapped a photograph of five or six little girls in white dresses in front of a Catholic church, all dressed up for a special occasion—perhaps their first communion. Fifty years later, while digging through his old boxes of mementos from the war, he ran across the photograph. He enlarged it to an 8 x 10 and sent it to the mayor (the *Burgermeister*, in German) of Ebermannstadt with a brief (or knowing my dad, not-so-brief) explanation that he had been an American GI and thought the town might want the photo for its historical archives, as most had probably been lost in the war.

The Burgermeister published the picture in the newspaper, telling my dad's story and asking the girls to write in. The little girls, by then ladies in their fifties and sixties, wrote or called in to identify themselves. The Burgermeister wrote back to Dad, thanking him for the photo. He also thanked him for liberating their town from the Nazis, explaining that before receiving his letter, they did not know which American regiment was responsible for their liberation. Finally, the Burgermeister extended an invitation to visit the town.

In 1995, Dad and Mom, then in their seventies, took the Burgermeister up on his invitation and stopped in Ebermannstadt during their one and only European vacation. They were overwhelmed by the town's response. "We were treated like royalty," Mom said. The town held a parade in their honor, hosted a luncheon with the Burgermeister and town council, and gave my parents a key to the city. They were even on the front page in the newspaper. Perhaps best of all, all of the ladies in the original photograph who were still alive attended the festivities, and my parents rekindled a sweet friendship with all of them—but especially with a particularly friendly and gregarious woman named Klothilda Blank. Dad affectionately refers to the ladies as his "Angels of Ebermannstadt."

Before they left, my parents extended an invitation to Klothilda to come to the States, and thus began an international senior citizen's exchange program of sorts. A few years later, in 2000, Klothilda visited and stayed for three weeks with my parents, who live in Rantoul, a small town in the middle of a cornfield in central Illinois. Tilda (as she is affectionately called) knew no English, and my folks knew no German, and everyone got along famously. She even stayed with us a week in Lake Forest to visit the sights and sounds of Chicago. We rode the train from Munich to Nuremberg, anxiously awaiting our reunion. Klothilda met us at the train depot with her wonderful German bear hug, leaving no doubt that we were welcome and that she was looking forward to seeing us as much as we were looking forward to seeing her. She was joined by her daughter, Daniela; an English-speaking friend, Angela, who served as translator; and Rhinehardt, a neighbor who was kind enough to bring his car and serve as luggage hauler.

We enjoyed a delightful lunch visiting with Tilda, who made us a delicious pork roast and promised to send me the recipe. After lunch, I continued my documentary film with an interview of Tilda and Angela, both of whom remembered living through World War II as children. As I asked questions, their memories came flooding back, and I nearly ran out of film, as well as tears. I wasn't prepared for the stories they were about to tell.

"The Nazis forced all the men in the town to join the army or be killed, leaving only the women and children," Tilda began. "We have a greeting here in Franconia-Swiss—'Grüß Gott'—that roughly translated means, 'God bids you good day.' The German people were no longer allowed to greet each other in the traditional Bavarian greeting. Instead, they were forced to raise their hand in the Nazi salute, greeting 'Heil Hitler.' But my mother refused to say 'Heil Hitler,' and she refused to give up her traditional Bavarian greeting. Even though my father had already been forced into the German army, my mother was scheduled to be deported to a concentration camp for 'proper Nazi training' for refusing to greet with the Nazi salute, which would have left us children all alone. Fortunately, a friend of the family was in the Nazi bureaucracy because there were no other jobs to be had. My mother escaped deportation because he reported that her failure to salute was due to a mental illness. In effect, he claimed 'She's crazy'—and it worked."

Tears were now beginning to well up in Tilda's eyes. She continued slowly. "My best childhood friend was Jewish. She was taken by the Nazis, and I never saw her again. And one of the little girls in the picture Dick took, Christina, was born without an arm. The Nazis would have taken her as well, because she was not perfect. But after the disappearances of some of the people, like my best friend, the local priest and the nuns decided to hide her in our church until the war was over."

Tilda snatched a tissue. "The women and we children were so excited when the American soldiers came. When they marched into town, we were all gathered together and a bit scared, hoping that no one would shoot us. My uncle took a white bedsheet and walked toward the U.S. army line as a sign of peaceful surrender. I got my first piece of chocolate from an American soldier. They were all kind to the children. I'll never forget how good it tasted," she reminisced, in her Franconia-Swiss German.

"It must have been Hershey's. That's what we got once in a while," added Dad.

"After the Americans occupied the town, all the children and families received care packages and food," Tilda went on. Angela explained that her town, by contrast, was occupied by the Russians, and the children didn't receive any care packages or food.

Tilda's story continued. "We were afraid at first because the Nazis had told everyone in town that the American army would kill everyone in its path. So many of us had hid in the caves in the mountains, along with our pigs and cows." Tilda sniffled as she remembered how humiliating it was to hide in the caves with the livestock because of what they had been told by the Nazis, only to find that they had been lied to and discover how kind the American soldiers really were. "But, as we found out, they didn't kill anybody, and they treated us better than our own people did." We could hear the hurt of betrayal in her cracking voice. "Yeah, we weren't so bad after all," Dad quipped with a wink. "My father was a prisoner of war in a Russian camp. It had terrible conditions. Even after the war ended, he was forced to work in Siberia in a work camp. He eventually escaped with a Polish woman years after the war had ended. He walked the entire way from Siberia to Germany, walking at night and hiding in barns along the way because the Russians hated the Germans for what they had done. He finally was able to return to Ebermannstadt in 1949. He had been taken by the Nazis into the army in 1939 and had been gone ten years. I had never seen him. We didn't even know him."

Tilda explained with great difficulty, haltingly, and now nearly gasping for breath between each agonizing sentence. "My father was so traumatized by the Nazis and the war that he never showed affection to any of us children after he returned. I never even called him 'Father' until I was over twenty years old. We finally developed some semblance of a father-daughter relationship in my mid-twenties when he helped my husband and me build this home after we got married."

Awash in her own painful memories, and with tears streaming down her cheeks, Tilda sobbed, "Hitler robbed us all of our childhood, our innocence, our parents, and our country."

We sat silently for several moments. Tilda and Angela were still grieving their lost childhoods and the pain of newly reopened wounds (which I had unexpectedly ripped open—I felt horrible). I was overwhelmed by the enormity of what they and all their country had gone through because of one madman. I had never really thought of the Germans as victims before. All the textbooks and all the war movies made one believe that the German people knew of the atrocities of Hitler against the Jews and the disabled—not to mention the rest of the world—and were in full agreement with the Nazis in their attempt at worldwide Aryan domination. This was the first time I had heard from Germans their view and experience of the war. They longed for liberation from the Allies too. The Germans were just as much victims of the Nazis as the French and the English and the Dutch.

How could I have been so ignorant? Why don't they teach these things in school?

With a heavy heart, I had just begun to process the stories that Tilda and Angela told when three ladies in their sixties arrived at the front door for coffee and cake. They looked like cute little German grandmothers with short, curly gray hair and pudgy, smiling faces. I soon learned that they were Christina (with only one arm), Agnes, and Regina, who were also in the now-famous photograph taken in 1945. A tearful reunion with Dad followed as each one gave him an enormous hug. Tears of appreciation and friendship, remembered like it was yesterday, flowed freely. I was simply overwhelmed by the emotions that these friends showed for him, even after all these long years. Especially Christina, perhaps because she had the most to be thankful for. It seemed like her one-armed hug would never end. I thought she must have cried many tears of sorrow when, as a child, she was stuck in the basement of that church for years, not knowing if it would ever end. But now, they were tears of joy.

> *"Blessed are those who can give without remembering and receive without forgetting."*
> —AUTHOR UNKNOWN

Each lady came bearing gifts for Dad and me, as well as the children. The most memorable were the hand-knit socks given by Regina to Mom and Dad. I must have had a quizzical look on my face, because she explained, in adorable grandmother-like German, "I remember your dad and the other American soldiers giving my mother their gloves during the cold winter of 1945. My mother unraveled the gloves and took the yarn to make sweaters for me and my brothers and sisters." The hand-knit socks were a grateful reciprocation of the warmth once given to her.

I smiled. *It was just like Dad to give his gloves and freeze so that someone less fortunate could be warm.*

The remembrances of the small but sweet kindnesses during the war kept coming all through the day. I was taken aback, time and time again, by the gifts of grace extended to complete strangers. Even more miraculous was that these kindnesses, little glimpses of heaven, took place in the midst of what can only be described as a hell on earth. But what was completely beyond my comprehension was what dark and evil things must lurk inside of people to turn them into monsters who do such horrible and hateful things to complete strangers who have done them no harm. Then, as it is now and forever will be, war brings out the worst in humankind—and the best.

These ladies and my father share a bond that none of us will understand, one forged by the fires of war. But I am so blessed to be here to witness it. Given all the blood and killing and battles my dad had seen by the time he arrived here, these little girls dressed in their white first-communion dresses with white flowers in their hair must truly have seemed like cherub angels, sent to remind him that there still was a God and there still were things that were good and pure and lovely. And I am sure that, given the conditions of war that these little girls had endured, my dad and the other GIs were angels of rescue as well. They too, it seemed, had a divine purpose to let these little girls know that there still was a God, and there still was justice, and there still were good and honorable men who protect instead of oppress, and defend rather than destroy. The tears and the socks and the unending hugs these many years later gave witness to their angel connection.

I watched with amazement at the reunion of angels, like an outsider on a snowy winter evening looking into a warm window glowing with a golden light. I only hoped that I could catch some of their light. *This must be how heaven is.*

"In everyone's life, at some time, our inner fire goes out. It is then burst into flame by an encounter with another human being. We should all be thankful for those people who rekindle the inner spirit."

—ALBERT SCHWEITZER

WEDNESDAY EVENING, JUNE 2, 2004, SCHLAIFHAUSEN, GERMANY

There was seemingly no end to the surprises this afternoon. By popular demand, Tilda's fun-loving nephew Horst gave us a bagpipe concert, in full Scottish regalia, including a tartan of the Clark clan. Also by request, Tilda donned her traditional Bavarian dress, the dirndl, for us to see and admire. We ended the evening at a local restaurant over more beer and schnitzels of one kind or another. We bid goodnight to our friends and extended an invitation to our hosts to visit us in the States, hoping to extend the international exchange program created by Dad and Tilda to the next generation. I hope they take us up on it.

During the course of the evening, I was able to get to know Daniela, Tilda's daughter, who I found out was a baker. She attended three years of baking school to learn her trade. More importantly, she is a walking miracle—a survivor of SARS. She had the good fortune of knowing a German doctor with a physician friend in America. This American doctor sent over medicine when no medicine found in Germany would work. After two years, most of which was spent in a coma, she finally recovered. A bit more reserved than Tilda, she told me that before she became sick, she was outgoing and gregarious like her mother (whom Daniela sometimes had to "shush" when she became very excited concerning a subject she was talking about).

"When one is face-to-face with death," she explained with much wisdom, "if one happens to live, one lives much more deliberately, and every decision, whether large or small, is done with great intention."

I must be in the presence of another angel. Who else talks like this?

Her husband had divorced her during her illness because, as he told her, "I have no use for a sick wife."

Why are so many men like this? They really can be so self-centered and useless.

And so she had raised her now sixteen-year-old son by herself. "My . . . great dream before I die," she haltingly said with great seriousness, "is to visit America."

I had to think about that one. *Is it really that great? Can America really be such a magical place that the dream of the rest of the world is simply to visit it once before they die? I love America, but can I really have underestimated my country that much?*

I told her that when she felt well enough to travel, we would be honored if she would stay with us. At the sound of the invitation, her chubby cheeks turned into a smile and her eyes sparkled with the glow of angelshine. I got the feeling that we would see her on our side of the pond.

REMINISCING ABOUT DAD

"Keep on loving each other as brothers. Do not forget to entertain strangers, for by doing so, some people have entertained angels without knowing it."

—HEBREWS 13:1–2

THANKSGIVING DAY, 1974

Dad was teaching nondestructive testing on Chanute Air Force Base in the cornfields of central Illinois. That's a fancy way of saying that he taught x-ray testing of airplanes. His class included students from all over the world who were in the armed services of our allies. Consequently, we had students from all over the world at our house nearly every weekend for Sunday pot roast—Kenya, Ethiopia, Saudi Arabia, Colombia. Dad's heart was so big, he never wanted them to be alone so far away from home. I am not sure if Mother appreciated his invitations, since she had to cook and was no fan of cooking. But my sister and I thought they were wonderful. How else was a ten-year-old supposed to meet people from other countries and learn a foreign language while living in the cornfields? Dad could always count on us to be an enthusiastic welcoming committee.

"Well, you know, Neece, Mr. Garcia is stationed here for six months, and his family is halfway across the world in Colombia. So I invited him and Mr. Gonzalez in my class to come over for Thanksgiving," Dad said, introducing me to one of his students. He always called me Neece when I was younger—short for Denise, my middle name.

My sister and I smiled, knowing we could soon add Spanish to the Swahili and Arabic we had picked up from our other guests.

THURSDAY, JUNE 3, 2004, BONN, GERMANY

"Turn from evil and do good; seek peace and pursue it."

—PSALM 34:14

Our delightful hosts gave us an early morning breakfast and an escort to the train in Nuremberg, which we took to Bonn. Our mission for this stop was to see the bridgehead at Remagen, which Dad's outfit, the 9th Armored Division, 27th Infantry Battalion, had taken from the Nazis on March 7, 1945. Daniela knew the battle well, as it was a hard-fought battle in Germany. Not being a student of war or military history, I knew only what my father had told me, which, of course, wasn't much.

We stuffed our bags in lockers at the train station at Bonn and headed off to Remagen on a short commuter train. The Ludendorff Railroad Bridge, known by English speakers in World War II as the Bridge at Remagen, was built in WWI and, in its day, must have been spectacular. The remains, two huge pillars at either side of the Rhine River, had been transformed into the *Friedensmuseum*, the Peace Museum, by the local Burgermeister and townspeople. On the south pillar flew the American flag; on the north, the flag of Germany. Fully aware of the death and destruction that a former generation of Germans had imposed upon the world (indeed, a large placard listed the death toll of World War II in the European Theatre country by country, totaling some fifty-five million soldiers and civilians), the present-day generation was determined never to return to those ways.

In an effort to encourage peace, a group of local schoolchildren had even enclosed in a bronze box the names of those who died in the battle, names which had been previously exposed on a placard. I have been to many memorials in my time, but I have never been to one where the names of the fallen have been purposefully hidden. Quite the contrary, in London it seems like every few feet a round brass memorial two feet in diameter has been placed in the pavement, making an announcement something like, "This place, in 1944, was struck by enemy fire."

The memorials serve as a constant reminder, and reinforcement, of old enmities and old enemies. And of course, in the United States every battleground of the Civil War reminds us of our wounded. The Vietnam War Memorial in Washington, DC has the name of every fallen soldier. Unlike other countries which place the names of those fallen in battle on memorials for the world to see, a reminder of those who have been killed—as well as of those who killed them—these Germans chose to put the painful memories in a box that cannot be opened and to move forward toward peace. It is probably a good collective approach to a painful past that no one knows quite what to do with.

Perhaps individually, we too can learn from this example. To seek peace and pursue it, we must not perpetuate the painful memories of those who have harmed us, but move forward in a concerted effort to forge friendships where there once was discord. How else are we ever to achieve peace?

The founders of the Peace Museum seemed to know my thoughts. The theme in Peace Hall proclaims to the world: "Each day let us work for peace with our mind and heart. Each person should begin with himself."

In the museum, Dad retold the story of how important it was for the Allies to secure the bridge, as it was the last bridge over the Rhine River that the Nazis had not yet destroyed while retreating east toward Berlin with the Allied troops close on their heels. The Americans took the bridge on March 7, 1945. Although it was already badly damaged by German demolition attempts to prevent the use of the bridge, the approaching American soldiers cut the wires to the charges and the U.S. army was able to move enough troops and tanks and artillery over it to eventually win the war. Dad's division painted a sign to commemorate the event, an almost life-sized photo which was kept in the museum: "Cross the Rhine with dry feet courtesy of the 9th Armored Division." It was good to know they had kept their sense of humor (and a fair amount of chutzpah) despite the many casualties. The bridge collapsed ten days later, but the 9th Armored Division had made an important turning point in the war.

As we strolled through the museum, Dad explained that when they were in Belgium, the troops had no barracks and stayed in private homes. The families were poor, but they received an allowance from the government for housing them. He recounted how one day he had gone to a school which was closed because of the war, and had taken down the long curtains hanging on the windows and brought them back to the family he was staying with so the mother could sew them into clothes for her family.

"Do you still keep in touch with them?" I asked, pausing for a moment as we looked out at the Rhine from the second floor of the bridgehead.

"Well, of course," was his swift answer. And he pulled out of his wallet a folded, tattered, yellowed piece of paper with an address on Adolf Hitler Strasse in Verviers, Belgium.

"Have you been carrying that in your wallet all these years?" I asked in amazement, knowing that any piece of paper with a street named after Hitler must have been at least sixty years old, and quite sure that no streets in *any* country now bear that name.

"Well, yeah," he replied, with an of-course-I-have tone of voice.

He had kept in touch with this family for sixty years! It was yet another story that, up until then, I had not known. I now understood why he had wanted to visit Belgium on our trip. When making the travel itinerary, he had requested that we visit Belgium. I assumed it was just another beautiful European tourist spot, not knowing that he had hoped to see, for the last time, the family who had opened their hearts and their home to a young GI. Unaware of its importance and limited by time constraints, I had dropped Belgium from our schedule.

When I saw that address pulled from his wallet, I immediately wished I hadn't eliminated Verviers from our journey. But Dad never complained about the change in plans. It was so much like him—never demanding, always so willing to accommodate others.

How could I have been so selfish? Dad needs to see these people, and I need to figure out a way to make it happen.

After a stroll down the Rhine, we returned to Bonn and squashed all five of us and our twelve bags into one taxi to find our hotel and dinner. We dumped our bags at our vintage hotel and set off to find food. While we were contemplating our dinner options over a pint of ale at an outdoor beer garden, a kindly and friendly German named Wolf offered to assist us with the menu (after he noticed our surly waitress, who was less than helpful or friendly). Wolf explained that he was a professor at a nearby university. He also suggested we vacate the beer garden (although it was fine for a brew) and recommended an outstanding Austrian place, to which he escorted me so I could make a reservation with the hostess for our crew without getting lost.

The restaurant was charming. Tucked into a neighborhood of cobblestone streets was an Austrian chalet. When we stepped inside, we were with greeted massive hand-carved furniture with hunting scenes, deer and boar trophies hung on pine-paneled walls, and a lovely hostess in traditional Austrian dress. Wolf kindly made the reservations for us. As we returned to the beer garden, Wolf asked our reason for coming to his country. I explained our mission.

"Really? The Germans are so grateful for what the Americans did!" he exclaimed with delight. Immediately, he trotted right over to Dad to introduce himself and express his profuse gratitude, as well as the gratitude of his fellow Germans, for his efforts in the war. In his normal humble way, Dad accepted his thanks, and we chatted for a bit with Wolf and his lady friend. We then went on our way to dinner after paying our beer tab as well as Wolf's, grateful for his kindness and thinking that it was nice to feel appreciated by the Germans.

Other than our friends in Schlaifhausen, it was our first introduction to the gratitude felt by the German people for the Americans' part in World War II. We were a bit surprised, as we really did not know what kind of reception to expect. Were they still upset over losing the war? Did they all support Hitler in his quest for power? Were we still in unfriendly territory? Thankfully (and reassuringly), Wolf's genuine delight upon seeing my dad and his sincere expression of gratitude for liberating his beloved country put our minds at ease.

Our Austrian feast was as wonderful as advertised by Wolf. The food was delicious, and the atmosphere was, well, Austrian. Marty, in his usual manner, fell asleep at the table. After dinner we carried him back to the hotel for a much-needed rest by all.

Friday, June 4, 2004, Bayeaux, France
"I thank my God upon every remembrance of you."
—Philippians 1:3, KJV

To our surprise, we discovered that our hotel in Bonn was directly across the street from a rail station. We boarded the train in the morning and were on our way to Normandy, France, for the sixtieth anniversary ceremonies. As soon as the train crossed the border from Germany to France, Dad switched hats and donned his favorite camouflage hat that he typically wore, complete with his pins and badges for Combat Infantry, the 9th Armored Division with *Remagen* on it, World War II Victory, Army Sharpshooter, the Bronze Star, and the American flag (of course). The hat proved to be magic in more ways than one.

The hat first became useful in the Paris train station. We had very little time between trains, and despite repeated requests at several stations, the Germans either would not or could not make train reservations for French trains. As the designated tour director, I told the others to wait in one place as I scurried around the station in an attempt to secure seats for five on the train from Paris to Normandy. However, the ticket-booth lady informed me that we were too late and reservations were simply not available. Dejected, I walked back to our party to tell them the bad news, only to find four train personnel and three burly policemen carrying our luggage and escorting Dad and his entourage to the train for Normandy. Apparently, the train personnel had spotted Dad's hat, recognized him as a World War II veteran, and jumped into action.

Upon boarding our luggage on the train, the train personnel discovered that the train was full. Undeterred, they imposed an order upon the train conductor to open a separate compartment just for us. They boarded all our luggage, shook Dad's hand, thanked him for his service, and bid us a warm farewell and good journey. We thanked them for their kindness. I suppose it was then that we began to feel that we were merely groupies escorting a rock star on tour. Little did we know how that inkling would shortly turn into a full-fledged reality!

We were joined in our compartment by the director and assistant director of the French Red Cross, who were traveling to Normandy to ensure that all the proper arrangements had been made for the ceremonies and arrival of the veterans. One of the gentlemen was a former commander in the French navy, and we had a lovely chat. They explained that the French people made a distinction between the American veterans, whom they admired and were grateful to, and the present-day strained political relationship with the U.S. They were quite helpful, as the conductor spoke no English. We exchanged business cards, and I extended an invitation to visit us whenever they were in Chicago before we bid them farewell as they disembarked at Caen.

In the evening, we finally arrived in the town of Bayeaux, the one and only place in which I could find any available hotel rooms within a hundred miles of the famed beaches of Normandy. Thousands of visitors had swarmed into this small hamlet, which had adorned itself, as had the rest of Normandy, with the flags of the countries to whom they were deeply grateful—the United States, England, Canada, and Denmark. As we disembarked, we could see a huge sign on the door to the café across the street from the train station which proclaimed, "Welcome to our Liberators." It had the desired effect of making us feel welcome and appreciated.

As the evening sun cast a warm glow of orange on the horizon and a gentle breeze fluttered the flags of our Allies which hung across every house, every shop, and every fencepost as far as the eye could see, I realized that it was here where the people were most grateful to their liberators. It was here where French mothers sheltered their children in their basements while the fathers took up arms, only to die at the hands of the Nazis. It was here in Normandy where the beaches were littered with bodies and the sea turned red. It was here that tens of thousands of our teenagers came to die so that the French could live. It is here where they remember.

We met a jolly old Scotsman coming off the train who had been coming back to Normandy every year since 1945 and staying with the same group of nuns who had housed his battalion. He spoke fondly of the area's whiskey and calvados and joked about his bum knee, which caused him a bit of trouble in this ancient train station with no lift. "A little souvenir from the Germans," he laughed as he limped along.

I carried Mr. Macleod's bags down one set of stairs and up the other. "I brought my kilt," he proudly announced.

That explains why his bags are so heavy . . . uff.

After collecting the appropriate number of luggage pieces and matching them with the appropriate number of family members, I

Dick as a private, around 1939 or 1940. What a handsome guy!

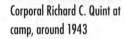

Corporal Richard C. Quint at camp, around 1943

Private First Class Richard C. Quint, around 1940. Always a patriot, Dad fibbed to enlist in the Army at the age of 17, in order to serve with his older brother.

A war ration book for Henry Doescher, Dad's grandfather. Everyone did their part.

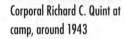

UNITED STATES OF AMERICA
OFFICE OF PRICE ADMINISTRATION

138289 AZ

WAR RATION BOOK No. 3   Void if altered

O.P.A.
INVALID
WITHOUT
STAMP

Identification of person to whom issued: PRINT IN FULL

Henry E. Doescher

(First name)   (Middle name)   (Last name)

Street number or rural route

City or post office   State

AGE	SEX	WEIGHT Lbs.	HEIGHT Ft. In.	OCCUPATION

SIGNATURE
(Person to whom book is issued. If such person is unable to sign because of age or incapacity, another may sign in his behalf.)

WARNING
This book is the property of the United States Government. It is unlawful to sell it to any other person, or to use it or permit anyone else to use it, except to obtain rationed goods in accordance with regulations of the Office of Price Administration. Any person who finds a lost War Ration Book must return it to the War Price and Rationing Board which issued it. Persons who violate rationing regulations are subject to $10,000 fine or imprisonment, or both.

OPA Form No. R-130

LOCAL BOARD ACTION

Issued by
(Local board number)   (Date)

Street address

City   State

(Signature of issuing officer)

BOOK 4

Geese on the Weisent River, Ebermannstadt, Spring 1945. Women washing clothes on the bank. What a peaceful scene after so much conflict.

Man on a horse buggy on a Sunday afternoon in Ebermannstadt, Spring 1945.

The original Angels of Ebermannstadt on their way to their first communion. Klothilda (the smallest one, in the middle), Agnes, Regina, and friends. May 1945.

Church building in Ebermannstadt, May 1945. The town had been liberated, the Nazi flags taken down; in their place, flags of freedom flew!

The Angels, in front of the church. Klothilda faces the camera. At first, the girls were afraid of Dad because he was a soldier in uniform. Always a kid at heart, Dad put a white handkerchief on his head to imitate the white flowers in the girls' hair, then danced around like a clown. Laughter trumped fear.

Always an avid photographer, Dad spent a spring afternoon in 1945 snapping some photos in Ebermannstadt. I wonder if these girls walking by the river are the Angels of Ebermannstadt!

American GIs on a Sunday stroll along the Weisent River in Ebermannstadt. Spring 1945.

A Christmas card sent from Dick to his mom, probably in 1943. In the upper left-hand corner is a stamp and signature, showing it passed Army inspection that no classified information was leaked (including the address, which was circled). Note on the bottom it was sent by V-mail, short for Victory-Mail. Perhaps V-Mail was the predecessor of modern-day e-mail!

Dad (on the right) with an Army buddy in Germany, 1945.

Staff Sergeant Quint, around 1945. Note the 9th Armored Division patch, Combat Infantry Badge (silver rifle on blue background), Weapons Expert Qualification Badge (cross), Good Conduct ribbon, American Defense ribbon. Not yet awarded at time of photo: The Bronze Star Medal.

Dad and a buddy taking a break on a field artillery cannon, 1945.

The Battle of Remagen on March 7, 1945 was a hard fought battle. The Ludendorff Bridge, a train bridge connecting Remagen on the East and Erpel on the West, was the last bridge standing over the Rhine River the Nazis had not destroyed in their wake as they retreated eastward. The Allies were able to capture the bridge and move tanks and troops East, toward Berlin, before it collapsed. Amid the rubble are handmade traffic signs in German and English, noting directions to Remagen and the few remaining roads.

An elderly woman walks beside the rubble that was once Remagen, March 1945. Miraculously, the Catholic church was spared from the bombings, and Dad and I attended services there in 2005.

stepped across the street and poked my head into the quaint café to see if I could hail a cab. As I inquired of the owner as to how one hails a taxi in Bayeux, I spotted our UK comrade at one of the outdoor tables already sipping calvados and waiting for a cab. The proprietor had already gone out of his way to ensure that our new Scottish friend got what I think must have been the only taxi in town.

Not realizing that we had our own veteran waiting across the street at the train station, the proprietor explained, "He is a veteran, you know. He gets the taxi first."

We finally made it to our postage stamp of a room. Having searched for available rooms for months, I was just thankful that we even had one. After dropping off our bags, we went out to explore the nightlife and find a place for dinner. Despite the thousands of visitors, we managed to run into some people at the local outdoor café and bar whom Dad had befriended at the train station. It was becoming readily apparent that there were few people my father met whom he did *not* befriend. Our little troupe was constantly losing him, only to find him engaged in a conversation with a stranger, completely oblivious of any timetable we might be on or the fact that we had been searching frantically for him. True to form, we were reacquainted with the definition of "stranger" based upon *The Dictionary According to Dad:* "stranger—*n.* a friend you have not met yet."

Watching him, I thought, *He loves people, and people love him. Isn't that what God calls us to do? If we can't at least be friendly, how do we love our neighbors as ourselves?*

We settled in at one of the packed tables on the street corner for a pint or two and to catch any breaking news of the death of another American hero—Ronald Reagan. Not only did we meet several veterans and their families, but I was also surprised to find several younger people who had come for the weekend simply for a chance to talk to the veterans, hear their stories, honor them, and pay homage to a grandfather or father or uncle who had fought. Each of them talked to Dad, shook his hand, expressed his or her gratitude for his service, and asked him to tell his story. After an ale or two (or perhaps three), we invited one young man who was traveling by himself to join us for dinner. He was a newspaper photographer, but he came here in honor of his uncle. He didn't even make a reservation—figuring (correctly so) that, given the average age of a World War II veteran, there was bound to be a cancellation or two that he could slip into. We found a small pizza joint, where the waiter also excitedly expressed his gratitude to Dad.

We are retiring early tonight, wondering what the next several days—and Dad's newfound stardom—will bring. I turn to Tom as we crawl into bed. "Dorothy, we aren't in Kansas anymore."

June 5, 2004, St. Mere Eglise, Normandy, France

"Be strong and courageous! Do not be terrified; do not be discouraged, for the Lord your God will be with you wherever you go."

—Joshua 1:9

"The 101ˢᵗ Airborne Division, which was activated on 16 August 1942, at Camp Claiborne, Louisiana, has no history, but it has a rendezvous with destiny.

"Due to the nature of our armament, and the tactics in which we shall perfect ourselves, we shall be called upon to carry out operations of far-reaching military importance and we shall habitually go into action when the need is immediate and extreme.

"Let me call your attention to the fact that our badge is the great American eagle. This is a fitting emblem for a division that

will crush its enemies by falling upon them like a thunderbolt from the skies.

"The history we shall make, the record of high achievement we hope to write in the annals of the American Army and the American people, depends wholly and completely on the men of this division. Each individual, each officer and each enlisted man, must therefore regard himself as a necessary part of a complex and powerful instrument for the overcoming of the enemies of the nation. Each, in his own job, must realize that he is not only a means, but an indispensable means for obtaining the goal of victory. It is, therefore, not too much to say that the future itself, in whose molding we expect to have our share, is in the hands of the soldiers of the 101st Airborne Division."

—Major General William C. Lee, address to the 101ST Airborne "Screaming Eagles," August 19, 1942

I am not sure what I had been expecting of today, but whatever my expectations were, they did not even come close to the reality of this awe-inspiring day. After walking in the morning to the gas station on the other side of town to pick up our Hertz rental car, we headed off to St. Mere Eglise, a village upon which thousands of paratroopers had descended in 1944, for the reenactment of the jump with some six hundred paratroopers. The small village was completely unprepared for the throngs of people. After waiting patiently in a line of cars for well over an hour, we simply abandoned the car on the side of the road, started walking, and grabbed the first bus we saw, which we hoped would take us to the paratrooper landing. With the bus driver and passengers speaking no English, and us speaking almost no French, we embraced our sense of adventure and just went on blind faith that the good Lord would direct us to a bus going to the right place! And, of course, He did. I overruled Tom's suggestion that we split up, knowing we would never find each other again in the masses. To our amazement, we were dropped off in a field where over one hundred thousand people had already gathered for the festivities . . . and more were still coming.

Dad, of course, ran into *more* friends whom he had met in our hotel lobby earlier this morning; they wanted an interview, a photo shoot, and to shake his hand. After several minutes, we pried him away and promised to continue the interview back at the hotel.

The entire affair was completely disorganized. Despite the letters from both the French and American governments spelling out where the ceremonies would be held and where and when to pick up credentials and passes (absolutely necessary to enter the ceremonies in which President Bush would be speaking) and congratulatory medals, when I inquired of the officials, no one knew a thing concerning what I was talking about. The tents supposedly housing the events were completely unmarked, and the American officials who were supposed to hand out the all-important passes and credentials were nowhere to be seen.

Nonetheless, we quickly learned that our ticket to everything was our veteran-turned-rock-star. Our lack of credentials and passes made us a "security threat," which was humorous with an eighty-two-year-old veteran and two children in tow. Nonetheless, we got our own private escort by an army private to the American army tents, where Dad granted yet another interview and photo shoot to the historian of the army. It was a hot day, and the tiny village café (which looked more or less like a barn) had completely run out of everything, including beer and water. When the kids complained of being thirsty, an army major with whom we enjoyed a fascinating conversation snapped his fingers and requested a specialist to bring us water from the army's supply. The major was in his forties and had been retired and happily living his life in the private sector when he was called back to active duty to serve in Iraq, from where he had just returned. When he received the notice that he had to return to active service, his wife remarked in surprise, "Do they know how old you are?"

A master sergeant who had been in combat in Korea and Vietnam swapped war stories with Dad. For two strangers who had just met, their conversation touched upon some very personal issues. Like a student wanting to learn from an older and wiser professor, the master sergeant asked Dad how he dealt with the fact that, like himself, he was a survivor of combat while his buddy who had been right beside him was not.

Dad matter-of-factly replied, "I don't worry about it, and neither should you. My time wasn't up yet, and neither was yours. We should just make the most of our lives." Leave it to Dad to teach biblical principles in such a practical sort of way to a fellow soldier. He is not a biblical scholar, but his heart knows the truths of King David who, during one of his many heart-to-heart conversations with his Lord, realized that "All the days ordained for me were written in your book before one of them came to be" (Psalm 139:16).

I am beginning to realize that the common experience of combat forges friendships out of strangers, even those who fought in different wars in different eras. While I'm sure the term is not original, I've dubbed it the "foxhole buddy" experience, and I suspect we will witness it many more times before this trip is over.

From the young privates to the seasoned officers, each one went out of his way to welcome the veterans, shake their hands, and express their gratitude for their service. Many we spoke with had especially requested the assignment, and when I asked them why they had come, each of them said something like, "Ma'am, it's an honor and a privilege to honor the World War II vets. They are a generation unlike any other."

(I really liked the "sirs" and "ma'ams" and decided that I should institute that in our household.) We became more amazed as the day went on that these young men and women would hold these old gents dating from their grandparents' generation in such high esteem. It simply did not seem possible.

A moving ceremony was held under the paratrooper statue "Iron Mike," a complimentary expression used by the U.S. Army to refer to men who are especially tough, brave, and inspiring. Any paratrooper landing here in 1944 would certainly qualify under that definition. The French dignitaries expressed their gratitude toward the American veterans and America. The American officials graciously reminded us all that we had fought for freedom and democracy.

Not one to be shy, before and after the ceremonies honoring the paratroopers, Dad struck up conversations with four-star generals and even the secretary of the army, Secretary Les Brownlee, just like he had done with everyone else throughout his whole life. He did ask, however, for a photograph with them, and they willingly obliged. Of course, he didn't find out until later that the person in the suit (as opposed to the ocean of green uniforms) was Secretary Brownlee, but it would have made no difference. He would have talked to him like the guy next door even if he had known who he was.

While waiting for the ceremonies, I struck up a conversation with the young soldiers around me, many of whom were going to or just coming back from Iraq. They looked as young as my son. One soldier standing on my left, a young African-American man from Alabama, proudly informed me that they were with the 101st Airborne. "You know, the Screaming Eagles," he said with pride—just to make sure that I was duly aware of the importance of their division. (I was.)

The Screaming Eagles of the 101st Airborne Division. Just the name gives some indication of the tenacity of these brave men who jump out of airplanes into enemy territory. First organized over a hundred years ago, and with an American eagle insignia, they are one of the most highly decorated and recognized units in the U.S. Army.

"Oh yes, I know the Screaming Eagles." I assured him that I, and everyone stateside, knew of the Screaming Eagles, and I thanked him for their service. "Yes, ma'am," was the predictable humble response to my expression of gratitude.

The most colorful characters of the day were two eighty-two-year-old buddies who were still quite handsome and were dressed in their original 1944 101st Airborne Division paratrooper uniforms. One had just completed two jumps last month and was quite miffed that the army had not let him participate in the jump today. They looked magnificent in their uniforms and were having the time of their lives granting interviews, signing autographs, telling stories of their mischievous behavior during their younger years, and smiling from ear to ear.

Despite their joviality, I could not help but think that they must have led difficult lives and that perhaps they, like so many others of their generation, were defined by the war. My suspicions were confirmed when I noticed that one had only partial or no fingers on his hands and no left thumb whatsoever—a souvenir acquired during his years in a Nazi POW camp. I had never met anyone who'd had his fingers cut off during torture. It's the type of thing one only sees in a movie. I let out a quiet gasp when I saw them. But like the rest of their comrades, they did not ask for sympathy. They were thoroughly enjoying themselves and the reunion. When I inquired about him, my new friend from Alabama nodded his head in the direction of the vets and proudly claimed him as one of their own with the 101st Airborne. "He's with us," he said with unmistakable pride in his baritone voice.

As we left the ceremony and parachute grounds, we boarded one of the buses provided for the veterans and their entourages, once again on faith in the hopes that it would take us back to town. Our bus was directly behind the ones with the Airborne insignia. As the buses filled with veterans left the grounds, the thousands of active soldiers on the ground waved, parted to allow the buses through, and then stood at attention and saluted the veterans on the buses. The unexpected outpouring of respect and honor for our old vets, which I'd witnessed all day from the active-duty soldiers and which now culminated with the salute as they left, was simply overpowering. I fought back tears and the lump that suddenly found itself in my throat.

We soon found out that once again, we were interlopers—this time on a tour bus. Fortunately, since Dad was a vet, no one seemed to mind that we were not official members of their tour group. As our bus entered the town of St. Mere Eglise in the caravan of buses decorated with the Airborne insignia and carrying Airborne World War II veterans, the townspeople waved and cheered, waving American flags from houses adorned with American flags of all sizes.

Along with the others on the bus, I was surprised and delighted at the outpouring of gratitude and pro-American sentiment. As we drove through the countryside and towns in Normandy that weekend, nearly every house, hotel, shop, and doorpost flew an American flag. There were more American flags flying than French flags. Indeed, many houses displayed only an American flag, while others had both American and French, and still others displayed a smorgasbord of the Allied flags, and even that of Germany—a country which had been invited for the first time to the festivities. Despite the invitation, I did not run into a single German. Not surprising, really—I think one would have felt very strangely out of place.

We hoped to get some food for the kids and relax when we finally made it to town, as the little café by the paratrooper landing was completely unprepared for the masses and had run out of both food and drink. But Dad was quickly spotted and asked to conduct yet another official interview, this one for future military training. During the interview, he quite humbly explained that he had signed up for the army in 1939 when he was only seventeen (and not even legally old enough to enlist), but that he had fibbed about his age so that he could join with his older brother, Phillip. I knew that before enlisting, he had run away at thirteen from an alcoholic mother, a truck-driver father who was never home, and eleven brothers and sisters. He had headed west, riding the rail cars, to be a cowboy. Going as far west as he could, he ended up outside Modesto, California, at the ranch of Roy Triplett, who became a father figure. At 6'2" and 140 pounds, Dad was called "Slim" by the other cowboys. When asked why he enlisted, he explained, "Well, I was hungry."

We continued our quest for official credentials and passes at the official U.S. Army locations in town, but were met with dumbfounded looks. We decided to try again in earnest tomorrow. As we attempted to tour the town, which was packed with parade-goers, celebrations, and concerts, Dad was surrounded at all times by people—fans, I guess you'd call them—ranging from five to fifty; mostly French, British, and American; wanting autographs and expressing thanks for his service. Many noticed his 1st Infantry pin—"The Big Red 1," as it was called—designating the infantry division that landed on Omaha Beach on D-Day. In his folksy, friendly, and humble way, he explained, "Well, I was not there with the first wave on June 6, 1944, but I came with a replacement battalion on June 12." He was always careful to give credit to the troops who came before him, as well as to the men and women who stayed stateside and helped the war efforts in the shipyards and factories.

People also noticed his 9th Infantry Battalion pin, and when he was asked, he unassumingly told the story of the bridge at Remagen. It was apparent from listening to him and to the many other veterans telling their stories that they did not see themselves as having done anything special or out of the ordinary. To the contrary, each one saw himself as simply one out of millions of people who had tirelessly contributed to the war efforts. These reluctant superstars did not view themselves as heroes, but just as regular guys who were only doing their duty.

Some unlikely-looking fans of these octogenarians, two punk-style Brits in their early twenties with tattoos and wild red hair, enthusiastically greeted Dad and expressed their thanks to him and America for helping out the Brits. They proclaimed him "AWESOME!" and stated that their goal was to get as many autographs of World War II veterans as could fit on the World War II replica U.S. Army outfits they were wearing. Completely unfazed by their unusual looks, Dad graciously accepted their thanks. He signed an open patch of space on their fatigues and modestly returned the compliment. "We couldn't have done it without the help of your boys. I sure am thankful for the British." The punkers joked and chatted with the man sixty years their senior, and then were off with boundless energy and enthusiasm to get the next story and the next autograph.

After several similar episodes with a variety of people (but none as uniquely attired as the punkers), we finally acknowledged that our status on this trip was merely to carry Dad's baggage. He was the star; we were the road crew. We all found an unkempt curb to sit on for the duration of the evening while our lead act signed autographs, posed for pictures, and answered questions, surrounded at all times by at least ten to fifteen people wanting their brush with a real live World War II veteran. My husband, a former corporate executive who had grown accustomed to regular VIP treatment, just grinned at me and sat down with the rest of us on the littered curb, resigning himself to his demoted status and incredulous, as we all were, at the well-deserved attention that the vets were finally getting after so many years.

*"No one who achieves success does so without the help of others.
The wise and confident acknowledge this help with gratitude."*

—ALFRED NORTH WHITEHEAD

SUNDAY, JUNE 6, 2004, OMAHA BEACH

*"Soldiers, Sailors and Airmen of the Allied Expeditionary
Force! You are about to embark upon the Great Crusade, toward
which we have striven these many months. The eyes of the world
are upon you. The hopes and prayers of liberty-loving people
everywhere march with you. In company with our brave Allies
and brothers-in-arms on other Fronts, you will bring about the
destruction of the German war machine, the elimination of Nazi
tyranny over the oppressed peoples of Europe, and security for
ourselves in a free world. Your task will not be an easy one. Your
enemy is well trained, well equipped and battle-hardened. He
will fight savagely. But this is the year 1944! Much has happened
since the Nazi triumphs of 1940–41. The United Nations have
inflicted upon the Germans great defeats, in open battle, man-
to-man. Our air offensive has seriously reduced their strength in
the air and their capacity to wage war on the ground. Our Home
Fronts have given us an overwhelming superiority in weapons
and munitions of war, and placed at our disposal great reserves
of trained fighting men. The tide has turned! The free men of the
world are marching together to Victory! I have full confidence
in your courage, devotion to duty and skill in battle. We will
accept nothing less than full Victory! Good Luck! And let us all
beseech the blessing of Almighty God upon this great and noble
undertaking."*

—**GENERAL DWIGHT EISENHOWER TO THE ALLIED FORCES,**
JUNE 6, 1944

We awoke at five a.m. for an early start to Omaha Beach, where the official ceremonies were being held at the American cemetery. Our first goal was to procure the necessary passes and credentials required for all the official ceremonies. Despite the official letter from the Defense Department as to the times and locations for obtaining the coveted passes on the previous day, like many things with the military, the plan did not match up with the reality. And no one in the army seemed to know the reason for the mix-up or how to get the passes.

The Defense Department letter had indicated a location to obtain passes, but after parking our car and walking about two miles to the entry point, the army MP guarding the entry informed us that the location to pick up the passes was *inside* the secured zone, but that passes were needed to get *into* the secured zone. To obtain the passes, the MP informed us that we would all have to walk back the way we had come. He named a destination which he could neither give us directions to nor knew anything about. We explained that we could not make an eighty-two-year-old vet and a five-year-old boy make another two-mile walk and then drive to an unknown location to which no one, including the MP, could give us directions. "I have my orders, ma'am." Veteran or no veteran, he wouldn't budge.

Feeling a bit discouraged and running out of options, I knew I needed to be resourceful to get ourselves into the ceremonies, but how? Just at that moment, God provided, and not a minute too soon. I spotted a group of four officers walking shoulder to shoulder toward us on their way to the ceremonies. Having grown up on a military base, I quickly recognized the brass as a colonel, two majors, and a master sergeant. If we were ever to get in, I knew this would be our only chance.

I boldly approached the highest-ranking officer, the colonel, apologized for bothering him with such triviality, and explained our plight. The colonel took a look at my dad with his assorted medals and proclaimed, "This man was here in '44! We need to do something for him. He deserves it. We owe it to him!"

He whisked Dad away with his cadre of officers in a chauffeured van and promised to do what he could. We sat down on the curb ready for a long wait. As long as Dad could make it to the ceremonies, that was all that mattered, and we were prepared to spend the day hanging out in an undefined location (perhaps a bar?) if Dad could make it in.

Surprisingly, in about twenty minutes Dad reappeared, chauffeured by an army specialist, with passes in hand for everyone. He recounted the colonel's words to the pass distributor upon noticing his 9th Armored Division pin: "This man took the bridge at Remagen! We have to do something for him!"

"At least he knows his military history," quipped Dad.

Magic passes in hand, we all shuffled past the unhelpful MP, who remained completely unflappable, and were chauffeured up to the next long line to wait for a security check. Marty still had a small pocket knife in his pocket that he had received the previous day with the 101st Airborne insignia on it. This caused a bit of uncertainty and concern on our part when it was discovered by the security check. Understanding that we posed no real threat to national security, and realizing the treasure of a five-year-old boy, the security official handed the knife back to him and just told him to keep it in his pocket. After the security check and a short walk, we arrived at the cemetery.

The view was breathtaking. Almost ten thousand white crosses and Stars of David stood on a blanket of pristine green velvet as far as the eye could see, each one perfectly aligned, and each one decorated with an American and French flag. The cemetery sat upon a bluff overlooking the beaches. The sun shone brilliantly, such that the white crosses and Stars of David glowed with an almost supernatural radiance. The breeze off the ocean coated our faces with a light mist. The only sound was the lapping of the waves, which reflected the sun like thousands of stars in an endless sea of blue. Veterans and their families slowly walked the length of the cemetery to their seats, in silence and filled with memories.

We took our place somewhere in the middle of the crowd of seats, about two football fields from the speaker's podium, and soon found ourselves engaged in a conversation with some fellow Harley-Davidson bikers who had ridden their bikes all the way from their naval station in Naples, Italy for the event. The military tried to make sure that the veterans were in front, so by and by, a specialist brought Dad and I to two open seats within one-half a football field from the front. In a few minutes I was also bumped, but I gladly surrendered my newly assigned seat to another veteran. I took my place standing on the sidelines, where I once again ran into our new officer friends who had helped us get passes. I thanked them profusely and learned that the master sergeant had just returned from Iraq. Upon listening to his description (which he gave without revealing any military secrets, of course), I agreed that it must have been a "hellhole." The colonel praised me for my "chutzpah" in approaching them on behalf of my dad. I (reluctantly) admitted that, as a lawyer, I'm often required to have a certain amount of resourcefulness and chutzpah—an admission which drew some laughter from the crowd.

The ceremonies were running about forty-five minutes behind schedule. While waiting, the American lady next to me took the time to tell everyone around her that she thought evangelical Christians were as dangerous and evil as the fundamentalist Muslims in Afghanistan and Iraq. When she discovered the gentleman whom she was talking to was an evangelical Christian, she apologized if she had offended anyone—and then continued to lambaste Christians. As a Christian, I *was* offended at the comparison of a religion whose primary tenet is "love others as you love yourself" to one whose adherents regularly strap on suicide bombs to "kill the infidels." Silently, I seriously questioned the intelligence and judgment of someone who could not distinguish between a religion whose members had founded hospitals, the Red Cross, the Salvation Army, and the very country that allowed her the freedom to speak so openly against this religion, with one whose members imprisoned women in burkas and beat them within an inch of their lives if they appeared in public without a man, who were responsible for the bombings of September 11, 2001, and who inspired children as young as twelve on a daily basis to kill innocent folks.

I offered my support to the gentleman with whom she was now debating. However, against my instincts to argue and defend my faith from her attacks, I remembered the admonishment of St. Paul not to enter into frivolous arguments and decided not to bother with this woman, who was obviously not open to any ideas but her own, however misinformed or ill conceived they were.

Presidents Bush and Chirac arrived by helicopter. President Chirac gave what I'm sure was a moving speech, but since it was all in French, very few of us Americans could fully appreciate it. That was no surprise, since Chirac is no big fan of Americans or of President Bush. *It is just like him to give a speech to Americans in French, even though he is fully capable of making the speech in English.* I was a bit peeved at the snub. We all listened quietly and clapped politely. After Chirac spoke, President Bush took the podium to a hearty welcome. He spoke of America's long friendship with the French and of democracy, he praised the veterans for their heroism, and he told how, in 1944, so many bodies, when retrieved, had Bibles on them. He stated that our nation was founded on biblical principles, one of which so aptly applied to those buried there: "No greater love hath any man than this: that a man would lay down his life for a friend."

I thought of the lady who had lambasted the Christian faith and wondered what her reaction was to this obviously Christian president. He ended his speech by praising the brave soldiers who had fought so hard to help the French, and proclaimed that if needed, "We'd do it again!"

The lump, which was now familiar, came back in my throat at the thought of sending my son to fight another world war. *Oh God, I hope we never have to do it again. And I sure don't want Donny to go to war—he's too sweet. He'd get killed in the first thirty seconds of combat.*

My eyes filled with tears at the thought of the sacrifice of so many for freedom, as well as the horrifying thought of having to do it again if world events called for it. It's one thing to hear about and think about history and events that took place. It's another thing to apply those thoughts to *our* future and *our* family. For those of us who have never experienced war on a worldwide scale, Bush's words brought home the reality that no generation is safe from the threat of evil and war, and that *our* men and women of *this* generation may be called upon to defend our freedoms and relive the unbelievably horrific stories I have heard over the past week.

As everyone started shuffling out, one kindly older veteran patted me on the shoulder and admitted, "I have tears in my eyes too."

"Thanks," I said sheepishly. *I'm glad I'm not the only softie.* I started talking with him and his buddy and their wives. His friend, I discovered, was Harrison Young, the Korean war veteran who portrayed the older Private Ryan in the movie *Saving Private Ryan*. After a second or so, I recognized the familiar face and said "My goodness, you are!" I had watched the movie one Memorial Day in honor of the veterans. Just from watching the movie, I felt like I had suffered post-traumatic stress disorder! And now I was here with the very men who had fought. Dad had said the real thing was very much like the movie. I wondered how anyone could return to a normal life after such an experience. I thanked him for his service, after which he graciously posed for a photo for me. I tried not to act too starstruck and bid them an enjoyable day, then tried to find the rest of the group in the sea of people.

I usually look for Dad's telltale hat to find him, but it seemed like every veteran had a hat like his, so it was hard to pick him out in a crowd. After some searching, I finally located Dad. We then found Marty, who had fallen asleep during the two-hour ceremony, lying under the chairs. The others were occupied listening to a small *a capella* choir from the Dallas Police Department. I took a few solitary moments to read some gravestones and say a quiet thank-you to those who had never left Omaha Beach. Each white marble cross and Star of David had a name, rank, and date of death. The stars also had stones on them, which someone had thoughtfully placed as a traditional Jewish sign of respect. I read each one and whispered a "thank you" and a prayer through the tears that were trickling down my cheek. My mind was flooded with thoughts of the lives represented now only by these headstones.

Each one was a young man with hopes and dreams, perhaps a sweetheart, and family who loved him. I thought of Dad's commanding officer—Dad just told me today that he committed suicide after they disembarked on the beach. I couldn't even imagine the horrors that each person had to endure—so much that, to him, death seemed the better option. Dad, as a medic, saw so many die. "In their dying words, they called for their mothers," he told me.

They came to fight a war they didn't start, in a land that wasn't theirs, to free a people they didn't know. And all we asked in return was just enough land to bury our boys. My God, how does someone do this? How do mothers live? The lump in my throat was getting bigger, accompanied by a growing nausea at the thought of all the bloody bodies slaughtered on the shore and in the blood-red water that day.

My time of reflection was cut short by the more immediate concerns of motherhood. Christy was nowhere to be found in the ocean of humanity, and a full court press was employed to find her whereabouts. Upon locating her, Dad and his groupies (*i.e.* the rest of us) spent the next several hours talking with other veterans and families, hearing stories of bravery and courage from these humble heroes who don't perceive themselves to be so, and meeting sons who had come to see the graves of fathers they had never met. We ran into the jovial old paratroopers again, majestic in their uniforms, still telling stories and one joking that his chopped-off fingers were "not much good for picking my nose." They still had the joy of life flowing in their blood. One of the army specialists presented Dad with a huge artillery shell from the cannons that had given a twenty-one-gun salute during the ceremonies. While Tom (aka Mr. Practical) was wondering how we could possibly pack one more thing in our luggage, Dad was simply beaming.

In an effort to keep from deteriorating into a puddle of tears like his daughter, Dad adamantly refused to walk the beach or the graveyard. I kept him company while Tom and the kids investigated the beach. We said good-bye to Omaha Beach and were chauffeured back to our car for the next event—a visit to Pointe du Hoc. After our less-than-welcoming morning from the MP, we felt like royalty with the chauffeur, provided courtesy of the army.

We stopped by a seaside town, Grandcamp-Maisy, for a bite to eat and a beer en route to the point. It was now afternoon, we had been up since five with no food, and we were all starving (and thirsty). While the kids played on the beach, Dad and I went in search of a beer. I know beer was not on my diet (doctor's orders), but it was a special day, and I figured a small celebratory sip couldn't be that bad.

After we located a café that would let us take their glass steins onto the beach if we promised to bring them back, Dad spotted an old chap with the distinctive light blue ribbon and stars of the Congressional Medal of Honor around his neck. For Dad, it was akin to finding thirty bars of gold. Dad introduced himself and shook the gentleman's hand, and the two old gents settled into a long conversation. The CMH recipient, Staff Sergeant Walter Ehlers, was escorted by two army officers, a translator, a news crew from Los Angeles, and his daughter. All seemed quite used to the attention that their celebrity charge was getting, and after shaking Mr. Ehlers's hand and thanking him for his service, I also settled in for a long chat with them and heard the incredible story behind his medal.

It was June 1944, and the first wave was pinned down on the beach. Staff Sergeant Ehlers was scheduled to go in on the second wave, but due to a last-minute change in orders, his squad hit the beach hours ahead of the second wave to find complete chaos. After days of coming under heavy fire from machine guns and mortar, during which time Ehlers managed to destroy two Nazi machine-gun nests, Ehlers's commanding officer ordered a withdrawal. Recognizing that his company would be picked off one by one without cover, Ehlers and an automatic rifleman moved to a high vantage point to shoot the enemy while drawing fire as their unit retreated. Ehlers was shot in the back, but managed to kill the sniper who shot him and drag his badly wounded brother-in-arms to safety despite his own injuries. After being treated at a field station, Staff Sergeant Ehlers insisted on returning to his unit to fight with his men.

The escorts, particularly the younger soldiers, seemed to be thoroughly enjoying their assignment and were amazed, as we were, at the many stories they had heard and the outpouring of respect for these former soldiers. The journalists promised to e-mail me their write-ups and photo. As we left, they all stood and shook Dad's hand and thanked him for his service. As we walked the beach, some local townspeople did the same—Dad even received a kiss on the cheek from one handsome gray-haired lady, which made his day. He made me promise not to tell Mom.

When we arrived at Pointe du Hoc, hundreds of people were milling about exploring the legendary cliff that the 2nd Ranger Battalion was charged with securing early on D-Day. Positioned between the Utah and Omaha Beaches atop ninety-degree vertical cliffs, it was a stronghold for the Nazis. The point still has the remnants of Nazi bunkers and gun stations, a sign that the Germans were extremely well-prepared when the Allies finally arrived. The entire point is covered with bomb craters, some as big as forty feet in diameter and twenty feet deep, that were by now overgrown with grass and provided a much-needed playground for the kids.

We ran into a jovial Japanese-American veteran who had been a member of the 442nd Infantry Regiment, composed of Japanese-Americans (many of whose family members were detained in internment camps) who fought in Italy. The 442nd became the most highly decorated regiment in the history of the U.S. Army, with twenty-two Medal of Honor recipients. Their motto was "Go for Broke." Dad mentioned that my mother had taught school during the war at Heart Mountain, one of the Japanese-American internment camps in Wyoming. I piped in to explain that Mom believed the treatment of Japanese-Americans by the American government was entirely unjust and deplorable, and she had quit her job as a schoolteacher to move to Wyoming and teach the Japanese-American children.

Surprisingly, despite the maltreatment of many Japanese-Americans during that sad period of American history, this gentleman harbored no ill will toward America or its government. Dad thoroughly enjoyed his conversation with this delightful fellow before moving on to investigate Pointe du Hoc. We also ran into several men who had brought their teenage sons for a weekend bonding experience.

One man, a World War II reenactor, gushed, "This is my dream vacation with my son. For payback, when I get home, my wife is going to a scrapbooking convention with the girls."

Are you kidding? You definitely got the better deal.

As we walked around the point, I tried to imagine what it must have been like that fateful day on June 6, 1944. It is no exaggeration to say that the beige cliffs shot straight up over two hundred feet from the small beach right at the water's edge. The hearts of the Rangers assigned to this mission must have sunk as they approached from the sea, knowing that their assignment was to scale these vertical cliffs while a rain of German bullets came down from the Nazis above. The few who actually made it to the top were greeted with huge guns, fortified bunkers, and miles of rolled barbed wire.

What were we thinking? It was clearly evident that it was nothing short of a miracle that the Allied forces took Normandy at all.

As we approached the edge of the cliff, a double line of rolled barbed wire was still around the perimeter. I asked Dad, "How did anyone ever get through—especially while being shot at?" Visions of a scene from the movie *Legends of the Fall* came to mind, where a young man in WWI was caught in barbed wire and summarily riddled with bullets from the Germans. His brother, played by Brad Pitt, went back alone into the German camp later that night and scalped the whole lot.

Dad explained, "Well, one or two soldiers would lie down on top of the barbed wire, and the rest of the soldiers would walk across their backs."

Yeah, as the barbed wire and bullets dug into them. At this location, I couldn't imagine more than one person making it up the cliff at a time anyway, making it impossible for one to lie on the wire and one to walk over. I was also trying to decide which was the worse job—being stuck on the bottom while being stomped on, cut to shreds by barbed wire, and shot at; or going over the top and just being shot at—but an easy target.

As I was having this internal debate, Dad began telling me a story, and as always people started gathering to hear an authentic World War II vet tell us how it really was. He said that the Rangers who scaled the cliffs and the 29th Battalion lost a lot of men, as much as ninety percent of their ranks. The crowd around Dad grew, and they started asking questions and requesting autographs and photographs and more stories. Dad, in his element, happily obliged. At that moment, resigned once again to our fate as groupies, we all found a nice grassy bomb crater to lie in and decided it was a good time for a little R&R in the sun.

Marty, a few days from six, yawned in a bit of a whiny tone. "There goes Grandpa again—signing autographs and being a rock star. Oi!"

After about forty-five minutes, we wandered on to explore a huge cannon encasement. As people bumped into us, they asked me, "Is that your father over there? He's so cool. You are lucky to have him." I, of course, agreed. "Yes, I am."

Before this trip, I really hadn't thought much about the "coolness factor" of my parents, or how fortunate we were to have them. They had gotten older and slower and had even started to smell like old people. You know, that grandpa-like smell. "Cool" was not a word I associated with them. It is good to be reminded and to see them in a new light— like the heroes they are, not just good old Dad and Mom. *Yes, they are . . . cool. How could I not have realized this? Forgive me. Yes, he really is a hero.*

The crowds gave way, and Dad was eventually able to continue his tour of Pointe du Hoc, but I was continually asked to take photographs of him with the various visitors—couples, families, dads, and sons all wanted their picture with the real deal. I overheard them rushing to the others in their groups to retell the stories they had just heard from Dad.

And each time I heard them, I continued to be astonished that Dad, who was just plain old Dad to me, was a hero.

On our way back from Pointe du Hoc to our hotel in Bayeaux, we wound our way through the two-lane roads that connected the various seaside towns and villages of Normandy. All of the houses along the way, from the tiny cottages to large chateaus, were proudly flying American and French flags. One rather creative family made an American flag with red, white, and blue crepe paper stuffed into chicken wire and displayed it on their fence. It was a warm welcome to know that our vets were appreciated as our little band of tired soldiers made our way back to our temporary quarters at the end of a day like no other.

JUNE 7, 2004, LONDON

"Build me a son, O Lord, who will be strong enough to know
when he is weak, brave enough to face himself when he is
afraid, one who will be proud and unbending in honest defeat,
and humble and gentle in victory."

—GENERAL DOUGLAS MACARTHUR

I had suspected that getting to the train station in the morning and dropping the car off at the rental place would be a logistical challenge due to the lack of available taxis in Bayeaux. However, the night desk person said not to worry. But my fears were confirmed the next day, and we set off as early as possible to drop our tribe off at the train station while I attempted to drop off the rental car and somehow find a way back before the train left. Once again, God provided our transportation.

I managed to find a kindly group from the British Royal Air Force who were gassing up their cars at the same station where I dropped off the rental car. I asked them to give me a lift. They cheerfully obliged and explained that they had spent the whole week transporting British VIPs, including the grandson of General Montgomery. I was grateful for their kindness, as it would have been a two- or three-mile journey and I was not entirely sure I was up for a run to make it to the train on time. In the spirit of adventure that I had fully embraced for this trip, I had already planned on hitchhiking if I couldn't find a lift at the gas station.

Apparently Tom was not as sure of my resourcefulness as I was, because when I arrived at the train station, courtesy of the RAF, he was missing. He had commandeered an errant taxi that had come too close to the train station and had gone to pick me up at the car rental place. It was nice that he was worried about me, but I had to chuckle—given how we had traveled through Europe primarily on my quick-witted resourcefulness, I took umbrage with his underestimation of my abilities to get things done. Truth be told, it was divine providence looking out for us the whole way since we had left the house. At any rate, he arrived with a sheepish smile on his face, as if he should have known better but wanted to be gallant. We boarded the train with just a few minutes to spare and were off to Paris.

I have to admit, I was shocked at the bathroom conditions when we arrived in Paris. The bathrooms at St. Lazare train station were filthy and didn't even have toilet seats! In addition, they cost fifty cents to use. When I didn't notice the one tiny sink at the end of the line of seatless toilets and inadvertently walked out, the bathroom attendant told me I would have to pay again to use the sink to wash my hands. I lost my temper and had a few choice words about bathroom cleanliness standards in developed countries. I ducked under the turnstile without paying, washed my hands in the sink (which had no soap), and walked out in a huff. "What do you expect? This is Paris!" she retorted in her French accent.

I find it hard to believe that Parisians think they are the center of culture when they can't even put seats on their toilets! The French have nothing on the U.S.

After the initial shock of the bathroom incident, we wandered in the train station trying to determine the next leg of the journey. We had a few extra hours between trains, which I had planned for sightseeing. Tom left for a few minutes (to what I thought was the restroom) and returned with good news. He had hired a limo to take us to Paris's must-sees: the Eiffel Tower, the Arc de Triomphe, the Louvre, and Notre Dame.

After a whirlwind tour of Paris, we boarded the Eurostar for London. We were excited to finally arrive in the British capital, where we felt a common bond with our English-speaking brethren. We all crammed into a classic London taxi with a friendly driver. Christy dutifully counted off our thirteen pieces of luggage and five people and announced, "All present and accounted for, sir!" with her customary report and salute. Our bed-and-breakfast was the Harlingford Hotel, a charming place in Cartwright Gardens, a neighborhood where I had stayed when studying in London in law school.

After lugging our bags (which seemed to get heavier by the day) up fifty stairs, we set off to find an English pub. I was finally off my antibiotics and had a hankering for a good ale and some fish and chips. On our way, we once again ran into an old chap who recognized the now famous cap with medals on my dad. The old Englishman thanked Dad for his service, although I suspect he might have had one too many ales himself. We settled into a local pub with a pint (or two) and some good ol' English pub food.

REMINISCING ABOUT DAD

"Clothe yourselves in humility toward one another."

—1 PETER 5:5

FEBRUARY OF 1986

I had just graduated *summa cum laude* from college and passed the CPA exam on the first try. I was working for Arthur Andersen & Co., the largest and most prestigious CPA firm in the world at the time, and had moved out of my Podunk hometown in the middle of a cornfield in Illinois to Chicago. Life was looking good. I was way too big for my britches. With all the arrogance of a newly minted professional, I said something derogatory about blue-collar workers and got a dressing-down from Dad that I sorely needed and will never forget.

"Don't you ever forget, we need those people. We need people to clean the streets and work in the factories and sweep the floors and run the machines. I don't care if you work as an accountant or work in a factory or work as a ditchdigger. I don't care what you do. But whatever you do, you do the best you can do. And if you work as a ditchdigger, by golly, you had better be the best darn ditchdigger there is."

'Nuff said.

JUNE 8, 2004, LONDON, CARTWRIGHT CIRCLE

"The depth and strength of a human character are defined by its moral reserves. People reveal themselves completely only when they are thrown out of the customary conditions of their life, for only then do they have to fall back on their reserves."

—LEONARDO DA VINCI

With a hearty English breakfast of eggs and sausages in our bellies, we awaited the arrival of Banita, our former governess of five and a half years, and her gentleman friend, Steve, a native of Manchester who had swept Banita off her feet and convinced her to finish her master's degree at the University of Manchester, much to our family's loss. Banita and Steve found the children and me playing hide-and-go-seek in Cartwright Gardens, a typical English garden, overgrown and disheveled and perfect for playing childhood games. As Steve said of Christy's laughter and loud squeals, "I would know that voice anywhere."

After a year apart, the kids were overjoyed by their reunion with their beloved Banita. There were many bear hugs from the kids, as if no time at all had gone by since we last were together. Marty has known Banita his whole life, as she joined us just a few days before he was born. He was particularly distressed when she left. "I want my Banitaaa!" is a regular sob whenever Marty is upset or hurt.

We were happy to have a native with us who was familiar with the underground. We collected Tom and Dad at the hotel and were off for a day of sightseeing. We toured Churchill's underground war room and Westminster Abbey and lunched in a quaint pub at Covington Gardens. Outside Westminster Abbey, Dad was almost nailed by a taxi coming, at least from an American perspective, from the wrong direction. After that, he obeyed the traffic lights.

As we came out of the pub onto the sidewalk, Dad's hat caught the attention of another World War II vet. The conversation that followed showed the unique bond that only brothers-in-arms share and a mutual respect and admiration for the efforts of their respective countries. A heartfelt thanks came from the Brit, who told Dad that he had arrived on Sword Beach. "We couldn't have done it without you Brits. You kept them at bay until we arrived," was Dad's self-effacing reply. With their right hands locked in a handshake and their left hands on each other's shoulder, their eyes met and a thin smile of mutual gratitude appeared on their weathered faces.

I then realized that World War II vets have a certain brotherhood borne from mutual adversity and the understanding of the gravity of the cause for which they fought. I have seen it again and again on this journey. They knew that losing was not an option. They had no choice but to rely on each other. Theirs is a unique bond, forged from the fires of war, never to be broken, and not quite fully understood by those of us fortunate enough not to have fought. The rest of us are outsiders, merely admirers of this mysterious and exclusive club. The club whose world-wide mantra—"Duty, honor, country"—was not just a motto but the entrance exam for all and the exit interview for far too many. On that sidewalk, we simply watched as two of this club's membership greeted each other . . . and remembered how they came to be reluctant members of a club no one would choose to belong to.

Although I should not have been surprised, one of the old newspaper articles in Churchill's war room was written by someone adamantly opposed to the U.S. going to war in World War II. "It is not our war—it is Europe's war," was the gist of his argument.

How similar the arguments are today. One would think the collective wisdom of society would be passed down so that we would all know that appeasing an evil dictator bent on domination and torture never works, and that the only thing such people understand is military might. They do it because they can, and no one stops them. Unfortunately, we haven't learned much from history, and each generation must learn for itself.

Dad was tired and turned in early—5:30! The rest of us found an outdoor pub and then watched the latest Harry Potter movie, which was especially fun to see in London.

JULY 9, 2004, LONDON, CARTWRIGHT GARDENS

I went out on a limb and tried Marmite on my toast for breakfast. I think it is the English version of Vegemite, an Australian condiment.

They are both, undoubtedly, locked in a tie for the worst stuff I have ever tasted. As a spoof, I told Christy it was apple butter. She slathered it on her toast, and we all waited for her reaction. It was priceless. We all had a good belly laugh, except for Christy, of course, who was already planning a way to get even. "You'd better sleep with one eye open," Marty warned us with the grin of a willing accomplice.

We started the day with a visit to Buckingham Palace to see the changing of the guard. The English are quite unparalleled in their pomp and pageantry, but I couldn't help thinking that the soldiers, with all their good-looking military dress, could never actually defend anyone with those ridiculous swords or run very fast with those tall boots. I told one of the guards, who was not supposed to be talking, that he looked quite dapper but that the boots looked very uncomfortable. He agreed. One of the friendly bobbies (policemen) at the palace said that until September 11, 2001, most people in London had such respect for the law that the police didn't even carry guns with them.

How shocking! What were they thinking?

We spent the afternoon touring the Tower of London. Marty, fascinated at the gore, spent the rest of the day saying, "Off with her head!" The Beefeaters took quite a bit of delight in describing the bloody details of the history of the place.

It continues to amaze me how cruel supposedly civilized people can be to each other. We certainly haven't progressed much over the past five thousand years.

We had dinner this evening at the delightful home of an acquaintance of Steve and Banita's. She was out of the country and was letting what seemed to be a multitude of friends use her house during their stay in London. Steve, a distinguished PhD who is well-known in international intellectual circles—not to mention a member of Einstein's Mensa Society—has quite a group of interesting and eclectic friends. One friend from South Africa, who was working on her PhD, joined us for dinner. As always with my husband, the topic of conversation turned to international relations and politics. It was a lively discussion—with Tom being just to the right of Genghis Khan and Steve being even further left than a Massachusetts senator.

At the end of the evening, we took the underground back to King's Crossing, hoping to see a train to Hogwarts. On our walk back to our hotel from the train, we stopped at a Burger King with a Route 66 theme, which I thought was a bit strange given that we were in London. I asked the workers if they had ever been on Route 66 (none had) and if the wrappers of English straws could be used as projectiles when blown like American straw wrappers. They were clueless as to this important skill. Being that it was late at night and I was in somewhat of a silly cares-to-the-wind vacation mood, I demonstrated by ripping off the end of the wrapper and blowing the straw. I shot the straw wrapper into the air and into the French fry bin, much to the delight of the BK staff and the laughter of my kids. Apparently the launching of straw wrappers is a uniquely American custom, not yet introduced to the Brits, who are known the world over for their exquisite manners. I was happy to be the first to set a trend.

JUNE 10, 2004, CHICAGO

This morning we finally started the long trip back home, via Toronto, on Air Canada. Once again, Dad's magic hat got him the royal treatment. I explained to our friendly flight attendant the mission from which we were returning. She found my father, shook his hand, thanked him profusely for his service, and planted a big kiss on his cheek. She then fluffed his pillow, brought a blanket, checked regularly to see if he needed anything, and generally gave him the best treatment in the house. He even got free drinks. But he liked the kiss best, of course.

The Toronto airport was a disaster. *Mental note to self: never, never come back to the States by way of Toronto.* Despite continued promises that our luggage would arrive before our connecting flight left, we finally had to abandon our attempts to connect with our luggage and catch our plane, hoping our bags would eventually find their way home. When we finally made it through customs and security and arrived at the gate, we discovered that Dad's magic hat had been left at a security checkpoint due to an overzealous security guard who obviously did not realize the significance of the medals and gave it an extra-thorough inspection.

We simply could not leave without Dad's hat, I explained to the airline personnel. As the plane was waiting, I sprinted the half-mile back through the maze of an airport under construction to find the hat, complete with all the medals, waiting at the security checkpoint. When I returned to the plane, I found that Tom (obviously suffering from a sudden and full-blown attack of Only Child Syndrome) was being given another complete security pat-down. Dad explained that Tom had lost his temper at the terrible service and luggage problems, and that the attendant, in retaliation, had required yet another security check. After putting his boots, belt, and other gear back on, Tom sheepishly boarded the plane, and we were on our way home—minus our luggage and Tom's bravado, but with the all-important hat.

It was good to get home. Mom sighed a sigh of relief that we hadn't been blown up by terrorists, her worst fear. Donny, tired of being babysat by an eighty-five-year-old grandmother who was not at all "hip" and who definitely did not like the looks of his long-haired hippy friends who stopped by, was happy to see us—maybe we weren't so bad after all. Dinner this evening was even more chaotic than usual as we each tried to tell Grandma and Donny our favorite stories and memories, so that we ended up all talking at once. It was a fitting end to an excellent adventure and personal trip through history.

REFLECTIONS, DECEMBER 2005

"You can easily judge the character of a man by how he treats
those who can do nothing for him."

—GOETHE

Months have now passed since our trip. Dad has settled back into
normal life again (*i.e.* life without a crowd asking him for signatures,
photographs, and interviews), consisting of coffee every morning at his
beloved local McDonald's with "the boys"—all retired World War II
vets—tending his tomato garden, mowing the lawn, sending toys to
kids in Iraq, and helping the neighbors fix whatever fence or piece of
machinery is in need of repair. No one has asked him for his autograph
in a long time.

I have had time to reflect and determine what life lessons I have
learned from this experience (I try to learn at least one or two big ones a
year). I suppose that I am most impressed by the modesty of these reluctant heroes who universally reject the title of "hero" and only claim to
be one of millions across the world simply fulfilling their duty for a
just cause. They are not altogether sure what to do with their new fame
after sixty years of obscurity and have handled it with characteristic
humbleness—a lesson for all of us.

I am equally impressed with the appreciation of the people of
Normandy, almost as if the liberation occurred yesterday. Because
it was *their* houses the Nazis occupied and *their* children who were
starving and *their* doorsteps that were red with the blood of slain
fathers and sons trying to protect their families, they welcomed the
Allies, their liberators, with open arms. And now, sixty years later,
many of them were able to do something I never could: peel back the
layers of time and see not an eighty-something-year-old, frail, not-
so-hip grandfather, but a twenty-two-year-old American soldier who

willingly volunteered to enter into a living hell to liberate a people he had never known and fight for a land he had never seen.

Despite the wrinkles, canes, and sometimes wheelchairs that come with octogenarian status, the hands of time could not conceal the indomitable spirit of the American GI fighting for a just cause. The people of Normandy immediately recognized these men for who they were: not saints, not angels, but scared young men who fought bravely in spite of their fears and changed the course of history, not only for Europe and the Pacific, but for the whole world. I thank these grateful townsfolk for opening my eyes to see these men as I always should have.

I suppose I will never understand why we worship Hollywood actors, who in addition to often behaving badly, simply portray other people who actually *did* something noteworthy. We *should* be giving homage to those humble, everyday heroes among us who answered when their country called.

And I learned that our vets and active servicemen don't get nearly the thank-yous that they deserve. They don't ask for anything in return for their service. But an unexpected expression of gratitude sure makes their hearts sing. Since our trip, I now make it a point to shake the hands of those who have served in our armed forces and give them a hearty thank-you for their service. The telltale military hat usually helps me identify them. I do the same for those who are in active service as I keep in mind this particularly anxious time for our servicemen and women. Whether retired or active, they are universally surprised by my gratitude and respond in the normal humble way of an American soldier, marine, airman, or sailor: "My pleasure, ma'am" if they are from the South; "No problem" if they are from the North; just a plain "Thank you" if they are retired. I hope the people in our country will make a practice of saying thank you to our retired and active military so they aren't so surprised when they hear it and know the appreciation of a grateful nation.

THE WAY BACK, AGAIN

SATURDAY, MARCH 5, 2005, COLOGNE, GERMANY

We are on our way via Lufthansa to Cologne, Germany, for round two of re-experiencing—or at least revisiting—my dad's first all-expenses-paid trip, courtesy of Uncle Sam, to Europe in 1943–1945. Last year we didn't have the time to visit some people who are very important to Dad. So we are going back this year as a sort of a farewell tour—I don't expect Dad will be back again.

One reason we didn't get around to visiting many of these people last year was that I had no idea who these people were or what impact they'd had on Dad. He seldom talks about his war years, and when he does, it comes out in bits and pieces. A short moment here, a quick tale there. Never a long beginning-to-end story with all the character development and twisting and turning plot that would tie together all the dots for me in a cohesive history of his life during the war. But once we are over on this side of the pond, the stories come like milk poured from a pitcher. And they just keep coming.

And so here we are, on Dick and Charlie's Excellent Adventure—no spouses, no kids, just Dad and me, for Dad to remember and for me to find out. (At forty-one, it is high time I learned.) I just hope that I can keep up with my eighty-two-year-old Pops. He seems to spring to life over here as he tells tales and remembers his younger years. It's a bit like turning back the clock. At home he can fall asleep in front of the TV in five minutes, but on the way over on the plane on an eight-hour flight, he was so wired that he couldn't sleep at all.

The stories started coming this morning over coffee at Heathrow Airport. I know when he starts, "Did I ever tell you the story about . . ." that I should just get out the video camera and hope to catch it, as his stories usually aren't repeated. About halfway through our first cup of coffee, he asked, "Did I ever tell you the story of when I was stationed in Belgium?" Out came the camcorder as soon as I could haul it out.

"My job was to provide replacement soldiers to the front lines. One of the perks (if you can call anything a perk in war) was that I had a jeep at my disposal to transport the GIs whenever they were needed. Me and another GI stayed in the home of a Belgium family with a girl about my age, named Marie, and her sister, Chloe. Their family was very gracious. Marie and I would have coffee and breakfast in the mornings. The government paid the family rent for the GIs to stay with them during the months we were in Belgium."

We are seeing Marie and her children and grandchildren on our trip. *I can't wait to hear her side of the story. I wonder if there was any romance there?*

"My group was forced to leave Verviers rather abruptly in the middle of the night on December 16, 1944, during the Battle of the Bulge. My buddy and I hopped in the back of a truck, but we fell asleep and found ourselves miles from the rendezvous point. We had to hitchhike back."

Dad also talked about another individual we were going to visit on the trip, Jean-Claude Hendrick, who as a boy of twelve witnessed the slayings of several captured GIs from the 9th Armored Division at the hands of the Nazis. Years later, he established a monument in his hometown in their memory, which he maintains himself to this day. *He must be quite a person.* I look forward to meeting him and to hearing his stories. It is hard to imagine living through a war as a child, harder yet to imagine witnessing the Nazis murdering the people who have come to liberate you.

Up until this trip, I had not even thought much about how blessed America is to have not had a war waged upon our soil since the Civil War. But for the Europeans, everyone has at least one family member who has died in a war fought in their country, or their town, or even their own home. Those who survive continue to tell the story to the next generation and the next. War and death are always present in the backs of their minds.

We are in Cologne now and about to disembark with a plane full of band members, complete with guitars, here for a rock-n-roll music festival. An interesting-looking crowd, that's for sure!

EVENING OF SATURDAY, MARCH 5, 2006, REMAGEN, GERMANY

We met an enjoyable and friendly person at our little hotel. He came from Iraq and speaks five languages. He is now the cook at this quaint hotel in Remagen. He says he enjoys using his language skills and helping people. He reminds me a bit of Jerry Lewis in one of his humorous parts where he plays a Chinese man with big teeth. We had a nice chat over a beer this afternoon while Dad took a nap.

REMINISCING ABOUT DAD

SATURDAY, SUMMER OF 1973

Mother was trying to raise a "lady," and I was having nothing to do with it. We had locked horns in a mother–preteen daughter squabble. I sat in the branches of the apple tree, away from everyone. I was frustrated and angry—again. *There is no pleasing that woman!* I ranted to myself. *No matter how hard I try, she finds something to criticize me for. There are two ways with her: her way and the wrong way. No matter what*

I do, I'm wrong. I guess I could run away. I pondered the possibilities. I had run away in second grade, but it was only for an afternoon. I had gone to Kathy Hanna's house and played Barbies before I came back.

"Honey?"

"Yeah, Dad," I said as Dad walked toward the apple tree. At least Dad was a kindred spirit. He knew something about butting heads with parents. After all, he ran away at thirteen to become a cowboy. I let him approach the tree.

"If you run away, let me know so I can go with you," he said, trying his best to be convincingly serious and not laugh.

"Thanks, Dad."

It's good to have a buddy, I thought.

SUNDAY, MARCH 6, 2005, REMAGEN, GERMANY

"All that is necessary for evil to triumph, is for good men to do nothing."

—EDMUND BURKE

We met up with Sergeant First Class Iva Rose Patterson at the hotel last evening. "Patty," as we call her, is a Tennessee girl whose father fought in Company A of the 27th Infantry Battalion in the 9th Armored Division. He was with the boys who fought in the Battle of the Bulge, who took the bridge at Remagen, and who went on to liberate several concentration camps. Patty's folks attend church with my sister in Gallatin, Tennessee, and Dad and Mom visited her folks when they were visiting my sister. Like most World War II vets, they made an immediate connection. Sergeant Patty is stationed near Mannheim, Germany, and like me, is on a quest to learn more about her dad's World War II experience. Unfortunately, her "Daddy" as she calls him, has Alzheimer's, and she has to make this quest on her own. But since we are here, she made arrangements with Dad to join us. We welcome the company. She told us that she has been in the military for sixteen years and that her next assignment will be either Iraq or Afghanistan. She reminds of someone, I just can't think who it is.

After scouting out the town last night, we identified the two main local churches and attended services at the Protestant one this morning. Of course it was all in German, and I was able to identify only about four words—God, Jesus Christ, and love. I suppose that's all we really need to know. The church was not at all full, and the congregation consisted mainly of sixty-five-plus-year-olds with white hair. I suspect it doesn't have many young people because there is no place for Sunday school (and none going on), and the music left quite a bit to be desired. It had nothing that would attract the younger crowd—unlike the more modern Protestant churches in the U.S. with their Christian rock music, lively youth programs, and multimedia presentations. The people were marginally friendly but did not go out of their way to make us feel welcome. Perhaps another reason for their small attendance.

After church, we hiked up to the Remagen Bridgehead, now turned into the *Friedensmuseum* or Peace Museum, my second trip to the museum in less than a year. Always able to find the pretty girls to talk to, Dad found a lovely woman of Chinese descent who grew up in New York but now lives in Bonn. Her mother worked as a translator for the United Nations, and she speaks fluent English (with a lovely English accent), German, French, and who knows what else. She was a journalist with the *Washington Post* and a Bonn newspaper when Bonn was still Germany's capital. Since the capital and all of its news reporting moved to Berlin after the fall of the Berlin Wall, she had retired, and her three small children kept her very busy.

With a journalist's inquisitive sense, she had lots of questions for Dad. She and I commiserated about the challenges of working and motherhood—which seem to be universal no matter where one is in the world. She shared that, due to low birthrates, the German government is actually paying women to have babies. *Where were they when my three were born?* She told us that she had come with her family to the museum because there was an article in the paper today about the history of the bridge.

As we were wandering the museum, I met another fellow, born in 1949, whose father was in the German army during World War II and was taken prisoner by the Americans at the nearby POW camp. Like so many others, he wanted to share his story. "My father told me that they were treated well because of orders from General Eisenhower to treat German soldiers as they would want American POWs to be treated. But when the American soldiers discovered the Jewish concentration camps at Dachau, Auschwitz, and Nuremberg, the treatment of the German POWs deteriorated."

I suppose I had heard so many stories of the German concentration camps and POW camps that I had never really focused on the fact that Americans must have had them as well. I also suppose that, after discovering the concentration camps, the American soldiers might have assumed that all German soldiers knew of them and approved of them and that the Americans took their anger out on the German POWs.

War does terrible things to normal and decent people. It turns them into monsters. Why do we keep doing this to ourselves? Are we ever going to learn? No, I don't think we ever will.

"At the end of the war, my father ended up in Newport, worked on a farm in the Midwest, and then spent three years working in France to rebuild that country." Apparently this program was required of the German POWs when the U.S. returned them to France. (I was under the mistaken impression that the German POWs simply went back to Germany.) "As penance for destroying France, they were forced to rebuild it."

My new acquaintance was quite frank and, amazingly, seemed to harbor no ill will toward us or the U.S. He said his mother and father married when his father returned from France, and they started their family in the Remagen area.

As I walked through this Peace Museum for the second year in a row, I once again saw the plaque on the wall announcing that the death toll of World War II, including soldiers and civilians, is estimated at an astounding fifty to fifty-five million people. Once again, it was overwhelming to me that one evil person could cause so much death and destruction. The words of Edmund Burke took on an entirely new meaning: "All that is necessary for evil to triumph, is for good men to do nothing." Apparently, too many good men had done nothing all the while that Hitler was building his power.

And then there came a time when Hitler was so powerful that the opportunity for mere opposition and debate was over, and good men had to die to keep evil from triumphing. Russia suffered the hardest losses—nearly thirteen million soldiers and civilians. Germany lost around five million people, equally divided between soldiers and civilians. The estimation of U.S. losses was 290,000—all military. In the Civil War, our losses took an entire generation, over six hundred thousand lives. But then, we had only ourselves to blame for that war.

The sheer magnitude of the losses hung over us. I can only imagine how many more losses there would have been had fate been different and the Allies had not won. As minds are wont to do, I imagined the what-ifs that could have been.

What if Hitler had won? What if evil had triumphed? Would good people have eventually risen up against him? Would the United States, already stretched thin in fighting both the European and Pacific Theatres, have been able to defeat Hitler without Europe when Hitler eventually attacked on U.S. soil? What would the world look like today?

The what-ifs were too frightening to fully contemplate, and I resolved that I would think about them another day, and for today, simply be grateful that divine providence had been on our side.

In thanksgiving for our blessing of being on the winning side, we ended the evening with a *Kirchenkoncert,* or church concert, at the Catholic church, which was built in 1147. The newest section of the church was added in 1902 and miraculously was not bombed during the war. The concert consisted of nearly two hours of classical music by German composers, performed by a men's choir, a mixed choir, an orchestra, and a soprano soloist. While the music was lovely, this church too was filled with white-haired seniors and almost no one under sixty-five. If this is representative of the church in Europe, and I fear that it is, it clearly needs a revival. Dad easily made friends with the seventy-plus-year-old person next to him, as I did with the one-and-a-half and three-year-olds next to me, the only children in the whole church—quite a refreshing addition, if you ask me.

After the concert, we found a Mexican restaurant for dinner. Dad's German is so bad (and embarrassing!) that I finally asked him to just speak English and let me translate. My German is dreadful and nearly nonexistent, but at least I don't make up words and shout them loudly. Consulting a German-English dictionary, as opposed to relying on one's memory from the last time one spoke German in 1945, is highly preferable. And Dad shouting out words that make no sense, like "*Brau!*" (meaning "brown" in German) when attempting to order beer (which is actually *Bier* in German) is downright in poor taste. But I guess I should get used to being embarrassed on this trip. Dad's not the only one. Being in the military and from a small, rural town in Tennessee, Sergeant Patterson can't seem to have a conversation (even with the Germans) without bringing up the Iraq War (which is not at all popular here, as one would imagine) and likening it to World War II. I really don't like to bring up the subject of war, but particularly *not* here, and I certainly don't believe this war is as simple as she makes it out to be.

MONDAY, MARCH 7, 2005, REMAGEN, GERMANY

More on Sergeant First Class Patterson. I have finally figured out who she reminds me of—my brother-in-law Ron, who grew up in the same small town in Tennessee (and who, by the way, stole my sister from Illinois and moved her down there). Patty is certainly a proud Southerner and, like many Southerners I have met, is an interesting study in contrasts. She is always talking about "Daddy" and "Momma" and "kin" and can trace her family back for ten generations. Every other sentence starts off with "My great-great-granddaddy done . . ." this or that. It usually has something to do with the Civil War (of course). Like many Southerners, she has two first names. Church is a big topic of discussion too—mostly about what denomination Daddy belonged to, what denomination Momma belonged to, and of course, what denomination whomever she is talking about belongs to. News alert: Baptists are usually involved somehow.

Patty has a bit of a know-it-all attitude, which can be quite annoying at times. Having forgotten that the reason the Good Lord gave us two ears and one mouth is so we can listen twice as much as we talk, she has an uncanny ability to talk at length on subjects she knows little about (like world politics, economics, law, business, stocks) and even more about subjects she does know something about (like Daddy, Momma, various kin, the stripes required for this or that military rank, which medals stand for what on their uniforms, how stupid her superiors are, her grievances with the military . . .).

Clichés seem to be rather useful to her, and she uses them early and often. I believe I have heard "Freedom isn't free" and "Freedom is always worth fighting for" about ten times already today. While I do not disagree, I'm sure that there must be another way to say it. Or perhaps I've just had too much history and talk of war, both past and present. I'm not sure why I'm so grumpy. Maybe I just need a good night's rest. And it's only Monday.

MONDAY EVENING, MARCH 7, 2005, ERPEL, GERMANY

"Oh say does that star-spangled banner yet wave, o'er the land of the free and the home of the brave."

—FRANCIS SCOTT KEY, "THE STAR SPANGLED BANNER"

Today is the sixtieth anniversary of the battle for the bridge at Remagen which, back in 1945, was the last remaining bridge over the Rhine. Dad woke up this morning singing a rousing rendition of "The Star Spangled Banner." He was in fine form. Sergeant Patterson dressed in her Class A uniform for the momentous day and carried a picture of her father in uniform during World War II. I was a bit nervous about how we might be received, especially with her army uniform, in what was once enemy territory. But I wasn't about to ask her to change. She and Dad had been looking forward to this day for months, and I was simply glad they took me with them.

After breakfast, we visited Kurt Kleeman, the director of tourism and museums at Remagen. He has visited with a number of veterans who have returned here. One even brought back with him the official army reports of the 27th Infantry Battalion that are now declassified. He gave us a copy of the report, and the four of us had a long visit. While we were in his office with the town records, one young lady was looking up marriages and trying to trace her genealogy. She was perusing the sixteenth century at the time we were there.

No matter where one is in this wide world, you always wonder where your roots are.

Herr Kleeman invited us to a reception hosted by the town of Erpel (on the other side of the Rhine River) in commemoration of the

Americans taking the bridge on March 7, 1945. He also informed us that the bridge tower on the Erpel side of the Rhine would be open to the public from three to eight p.m. It is open only once every ten years, on March 7, to commemorate the liberation of the towns of Remagen and Erpel by the Americans. Herr Kleeman also explained that the bridge and the tunnel were built by Hitler during World War I in anticipation of moving German troops for an eventual attack on France. He was certainly planning ahead!

In my continuing quest to understand the war and our present-day relations, both from a German and American perspective, I asked Herr Kleeman how the German people in Remagen felt about the Americans then and now. "Unfortunately," he responded, "Remagen was home to a POW camp in which approximately three hundred thousand German soldiers were held by American troops. This has colored their view of Americans." Apparently the conditions at the camp were not ideal, to say the least.

"Today," he went on, "I don't think the Germans and Americans know enough about each other. When Germans see films like *Saving Private Ryan*, they wonder if Americans still harbor resentment toward the Germans. The general view by the Germans of Hitler, however, is that he was a madman. But," he explained, "the country was under twelve years of his brainwashing that the Aryan race was the best and that it needed more territory. The propaganda started when children were young, in the Hitler Youth program, and continued to adulthood. It was the Depression, as well. People could not find jobs unless they joined the Nazi Party. Otherwise, they stayed unemployed and could not feed their families."

I assured Herr Kleeman that when Americans think of Germany now, they have a generally favorable impression, and that the Nazis and Hitler are no longer the first things that come to mind. I explained that

Americans might first think of German engineering or German beer, both of which we hold in very high regard. Sergeant Patterson piped in that we also like our BMWs and Mercedes.

After we thought we could politely take up no more of his time, we said *"Auf wiedersehen"* and *"Danke"* to Herr Kleeman and headed off for the bridgehead on the Remagen side of the Rhine, where Dad and Sergeant Patterson found themselves being interviewed by a local TV station. The wind whipped through the river valley, and both the German flag on the north pillar and American flag on the south pillar flew straight out as they spoke of the war under the waving flags. *It is fitting that the American flag is a constant reminder and tribute to the home of the brave who fought so that Germany too could be a land of the free.*

After their brush with fame, we boarded the ferry and crossed the Rhine to Erpel for lunch. Erpel was a charming little village with cobblestone streets going in no particular direction, ancient buildings (one had the date of 1607), and simple townspeople. We found a small inn, about four hundred years old, and settled in to enjoy some hot soup. I tried to buy today's newspaper, as it had a nice article about the story of the bridge. But alas, as I have found in most of Europe, the shop owners don't want to work especially long hours (or even short ones, it seems), and the only store in the entire village that might have carried a paper closed at noon.

On our way to the bridge, an older gentleman in his late seventies or early eighties noticed Sergeant Patterson's uniform and recognized that we were Americans who had come to visit for the event. His enthusiasm was unbridled. He rushed up to us, speaking only excited German, and we really had no idea what he was trying to say. I even thought for a moment that he might have been the town drunk, as he seemed overly excited to see complete strangers. I quickly pulled out my German-English dictionary. He asked about my dad and Sergeant Patterson. In broken German, we shared that Sergeant Patterson's father was a soldier in World War II and showed him the picture she always carried of her father in uniform. And of course, Dad shared that his company took the bridge at Remagen. At this, we just held our breaths, not knowing what would be the reaction of this former enemy.

His reaction was like that of an old friend trying to clear up an old misunderstanding—trying to let bygones be bygones and rekindle a friendship that for too many years had been silent. He shook our hands so vigorously I thought they might fall off. He told us that he had been a *Soldaten*—a soldier in the German army in World War II—and that his father had also been a German soldier who was taken to Moscow as a POW by the Russians. He seemed so excited to see a fellow soldier (even though they were from opposite sides) and to share his story with us. He seemed to know that we would understand that he had not wanted to fight for the Nazis, but like so many other Germans, he was given no choice. And he desperately seemed to want our friendship. He showed us his house and a picture of himself and his father in World War II. He asked us in for tea, but we declined as we were anxious to see the bridge.

When we arrived at the bridgehead at three p.m., there were already people waiting for it to be opened. As we wandered through the remains of what had once been a spectacular bridgehead, some of the older Germans recognized my dad's camouflage army hat. (Hats seem to be a favorite uniform of retired vets.) They asked about his service, and upon discovering that it was his division that took the bridge, one very tall and large German-looking gentleman with a tweed blazer and feather in his tweed hat shook Dad's hand with both of his and issued a hearty, "Thank you for giving us Germans our freedom. I was four years old and living in Berlin at the time you came. We were waiting for you!"

Another gentleman said, "This day you gave Germany our liberation! Thank you! Thank you!" Others simply shook his hand and said, "Danke."

Such heartfelt thanksgiving was completely unexpected, and we were taken a bit by surprise. But it was a week of surprises, and we should have been getting used to them by now. Their thanks was heart-warming to hear, and we felt very welcomed by these grateful people. Between our enthusiastic former soldier friend whom we had met on the cobblestone street and these friendly Germans, our anxiety over how we would be received melted away. By the end of the tour of the bridgehead, we felt that we were indeed in friendly territory.

After touring the bridgehead, we set out for the tunnel, which was enormous and went through the mountain by the bridge. People and families of all ages were streaming in to catch a glimpse of this rare view of life before their freedom. TV crews and newspapers swarmed the area. We ended up talking with a history professor from a local high school who was attending the event with one of his students. Of course, most Germans had never known what it was like to grow up under the Nazis, and this was a rare opportunity to see a portion of their past that is, quite simply, painful to remember.

Fortunately, both of them served as translators for another gentle-man who came up to us and excitedly tried to tell us in German that he remembered my father from his visit to Remagen in 1995 with my mother. This thirty-something-year-old, an obvious history buff, had made the 250-kilometer trip from his hometown to Remagen and recalled how Dad had signed a book for him ten years ago. He asked him for another signature on one of today's brochures.

Dad was thoroughly enjoying himself, and more importantly, now as an older man, he was reveling in seeing firsthand the fruits of his labor as a young man. When he arrived in 1945, the towns had been destroyed physically, economically, spiritually, and emotionally by the Nazis. Now, after sixty years of freedom, they were thriving and charming hamlets, bustling with people full of hopes and dreams. The words of thanks by these free and grateful people made it all worthwhile. Soldiers don't expect thanks for doing what is their duty. It was truly more than he had ever hoped for.

We finally trotted off to the reception sponsored by the town of Erpel by following one of the handsome newspaper reporters Patty had befriended. As we approached the reception, Dad was spotted by more press, and the mayor greeted him and directed us to seats reserved for us near the front, courtesy of Herr Kleeman. The room was packed with people standing near the back and sides, about five hundred or so. During the ceremony, a number of speeches were made by the Burgermeister and various local and state government officials. There were also some readings of diaries dating back to 1944. These were all in German and were thankfully interspersed with pieces by Bach (of course), played on the violin, trumpet, and piano. After the church service, the concert on Sunday, and this today, I get the sense that the Germans really like their eighteenth-century composers!

Finally, after more than two hours, the ceremony concluded with the national anthems of the United States (played first!) and Germany. Although I didn't understand more than five words of the whole ceremony, the international language of friendship, freedom, peace, and thankfulness came through loud and clear.

About midway through the ceremony, I realized that the last ferry back to Remagen on the other side of the river would leave well before the end of the ceremonies. Since we spoke almost no German and were having difficulty with our cell phones, our newspaper editor friend was gracious enough to call and reserve a taxi, which was waiting for us at the end of the ceremonies. Knowing that Dad and Patty would want to visit and linger, I convinced the taxi driver to wait and promised him a healthy tip.

Upon returning to the festivities, I found Dad jovially sipping wine with a former German colonel and Hans Peter Kurten, the former

Burgermeister of Remagen and founder of the Peace Museum on the Remagen side. I ran into our German soldier friend from earlier in the afternoon. He seemed downright delighted to see us again, and he gave us a hearty handshake. I snapped a picture of the two old soldiers, once enemies, now friends.

The Burgermeister of Erpel, who looked like movie critic Joel Siegel on *Good Morning, America,* thanked us profusely for coming. He explained that in his speech that evening, he had told how the American arrival in Remagen was seen as a good thing by the German people. The Americans were welcomed because the people of Remagen and Erpel knew that the end of the war was coming soon. He also emphatically shared with us that they, the people of Remagen and Erpel and the rest of Germany, saw Americans as friends. I was grateful that he took the time to tell us what was in his speech and happy that it confirmed what I had already surmised from the warm and fuzzy feelings I had.

"One of the most emotional times for me was in 1995 on March 7 when so many U.S. soldiers returned to Remagen for the fiftieth anniversary," the Burgermeister shared. "When I saw all those old soldiers as they crossed the river on a ferry from the Remagen side of the bridge tower to the Erpel side, it was an incredibly emotional experience for me."

I tried to imagine what a glorious scene it must have been as the liberators came to survey what the towns had done with the freedom they had brought. These soldiers had been stewards of the torch of liberty and had entrusted it to the people of Erpel and Remagen. They had come to make sure that their trust was not misplaced. And it wasn't. Although the entire town had been rebuilt from the damage from the war, the bridge, as magnificent as it had once been, had purposefully never been rebuilt—it was a daily reminder of what once was and how close they had come to losing their freedom.

There were a number of former German soldiers in that crowded room, each with a story to tell. And just like our soldier friend, each one made a point of finding us and telling us his story, trying very hard to break the language barrier. Although we might not have understood every word, we could hear their spirit, and their spirit was of friendship and thanksgiving and peace. One gentleman said that he was on the top of the east bridge tower (the Erpel side) when the Americans came through on March 7, 1945. His group was the lone remaining company on the bridge, as his fellow German soldiers had already retreated to the mountains beyond. We lost a few of the details of the story at this point due to our language hurdles, but in the end, he told us that he had escaped from the Germans to the American POW camp. He then spent some time rebuilding France after the war. Apparently escaping to the American side was preferable to what the Germans were doing (or were going to do) to him.

Each old soldier had a similar story. None of them had wanted to fight for the Nazis, but they had no choice, facing certain death if they refused or were caught escaping. They were thankful that the Americans had won and given them their freedom. I stood in amazement as one after another, after waiting in line, came up to us and shared with us their intensely personal stories.

Why do they feel compelled to do so, especially to us, former enemies? Perhaps they want to explain to someone—an American, a fellow soldier—their plight, in the hopes that we will understand and forgive and befriend. We did, of course, and countless hugs were exchanged that night. *Who knows, perhaps this is the start of a new era of international understanding.*

Exhausted from a long day and emotionally drained, we hopped into the taxi, which had by that time been waiting nearly an hour. We crossed the auto ferry to the west side of the Rhine at Remagen and took a short detour to McDonald's, still Dad's favorite restaurant, for a Big Mac and a photo op on the way back to the hotel. I dropped Dad off at the room and went searching for a newspaper as a souvenir for him of the day's events. My efforts to find one at the nearby *Bahnhauf* (train station) remained unfruitful. However, a kind young man from Egypt who was in the Bahnhauf overheard my plight and offered me a lift to the nearest gas station mart, which, as he put it, was my "last hope" of finding a newspaper. By this time I had almost become accustomed to God providing transportation at the last minute, even if it meant jumping into a car with a complete stranger in a foreign country. I accepted his offer, scooted away in the typical undersized and sparsely equipped European car, found a paper at the gas station, heard about his sister in Cleveland (it seems like every working person here has a brother or sister in Ohio) and called it a night.

MARCH 8, 2005, VERVIERS, BELGIUM

"My command is this: love each other as I have loved you."

—JOHN 15:12

We said good-bye to Sergeant Patterson this morning and took off by train to Verviers, Belgium, to visit an old friend (girlfriend?) of Dad's. The only town in Belgium Dad ever talks about is Verviers. Listening to him, one might think there was no other town in all of Belgium except for Verviers! And of course, the only woman in all of Belgium is Marie. When I had suggested during the planning phase of this trip that we (meaning I) might want to see Brugge or Brussels or Luxemburg, Dad was completely uninterested in anything of the sort. Indeed, he had so many people he wanted to visit scattered in tiny hamlets throughout Europe, there was no room for sightseeing whatsoever.

Dad arrived on the beaches of Normandy on D-Day plus six, June 12, 1944, and they were working their way eastward toward Berlin against the retreating German army. Dad and another GI were billeted with Marie's family in Verviers for several weeks during the fall of 1944. Marie's mother was very kind and gracious to them, and Marie, who was twenty-three at the time (Dad was twenty-two) has always kept a special place in his heart. While he was stationed in Europe with the U.S. Air Force in 1972, he looked up Marie, who was still living in the same town, and met Marie and her husband and family. Marie's eldest daughter, Marienne, and my older sister, who was about eleven at the time, became pen pals for many years. He visited again in 1995 with my mother. Dad had been looking forward to this visit, the highlight of his trip, for quite some time.

Beatrice Laurent, Marie's younger daughter, picked us up from the hotel in Verviers with her daughter Astrid, sixteen, who doubled as an interpreter. We visited the children's shop which Marienne owned. As in many small towns, other family members worked at the shop, and we met cousins, nieces, nephews, boyfriends, etc.—too many to keep track of. Marienne packed us up with gifts for the children and refused to let us pay for anything. We also drove by Marie's old house where Dad stayed in 1944, 53 Rue Aux Laines (or something close to that—but clearly no longer called Adolf Hitler Strasse as had been indicated on the crumpled, sixty-year-old piece of paper that held her address in 1944), and the large warehouse building where many of the other GIs stayed. (I think Dad got the better deal.)

Finally, we arrived at Marie's house. The reunion was absolutely joyful. We arrived with presents in tow. As we walked in the door, with Dad singing Irving Berlin's "Marie," Marie, eighty-three years old with white hair and an infectious smile, shuffled down the hallway with her arms open wide, simply beaming. They gave each other a big hug as the rest of us watched, caught in the glow of their warm friendship.

The entire extended family had gathered at Marie's house for visiting and eating crackers and chips and drinking wine and soft drinks. We

Dad and his bride, the love of his life, Jean Morton Quint, on their wedding day. June 18, 1960

With Dad on my wedding day.

One of Dick's first classes at Chanute Air Force Base, around 1968. Gary Ingle, a student Dad mentored who became a lifelong friend, is standing on the far left.

Never one to be shy, Dad treats everyone the
same (at least now that he's a civilian). Here he is
with a four-star general, surrounded by the 101st
Airborne at St. Mere Eglise, France. June 5, 2004

Dick at the Remagen bridgehead, with the
German and American flags waving in the
wind. June 3, 2004.

On his return trip to Ebermannstadt in 2004, Dad was reunited with his Angels. From left to right:
Agnes, Klothilda (in her beautiful Bavarian dirndl), Regina, Dad, and Christina. Here they are in
front of Klothilda's home, where an American flag welcomed us.

Seated: Gelda and her husband. Standing: Gelda's brother-in-law, Me, Dad. Dad's mission in traveling to Altenburg in March 2005 was to report back to Gelda that he had kept his promise to her mother to find her brother in Chicago. Dad rode a train from Minnesota to Chicago to carry out that promise.

Verviers, Belgium, March 2005. Maria told stories to her children and grandchildren about Dick and the GIs, just as Dick told stories to his children and grandchildren of Maria and her family. It was great to meet each other's families. Here is Dick with some of Maria's grandchildren.

Grandpa Quint, Christy, and friends from the 101st Airborne Division, St. Mere Eglise. June 5, 2004.

At the Remagen Bridgehead, June 3, 2004. In back, left to right: Dad, Tom, and Me. In front: Marty and Christy

Dad and Mom boating on Lake Geneva on their anniversary. June 2006

There are few things better than hugs from Grandpa. Here's Grandpa Quint with Christy and Marty in London, June 2004. Camouflage gear for everyone!

Dad and I singing "God Bless America" on Veterans Day, 2006, in Washington DC. This was the last trip we made together before he was too sick to travel. We heard George W. Bush speak at the Tomb of the Unknown Soldier and visited the WWII Memorial.

heard more stories from Marie and "Dick," as she called him. Beatrice's husband, Christian, soon joined us, as he came home from work and was quickly given the job of translator. Even the twenty-somethings and the teenage crowd seemed to enjoy seeing Dick in person, as they too had heard many stories about him from their grandmother.

> *"I expect to pass through this world but once. Any good, therefore, that I can do or any kindness I can show to any fellow creature, let me do it now. Let me not defer or neglect it for I shall not pass this way again."*
>
> —STEPHEN GRELLET

Dick and Marie instantly turned back the clock sixty years and didn't skip a beat. They continued their conversation like it was yesterday when they had last seen each other. "Do you recall the time I went to what is now called Aachen, Germany? I found a schoolhouse that was closed with tall windows—and on the windows were these long curtains and in the bucket next to the stove, there was a supply of coal? I knew your family didn't have hardly any clothes and hardly anything to keep warm. So I took down the curtains and loaded up the coal and brought them back to your mother. Do you remember?"

Marie smiled. She did indeed remember this act of kindness. It was hard for me to imagine schools being closed and not having any clothes or a warm home. But then it was war, and it is hard to imagine war, too, when one has not been through it. But it was easy to imagine Dad thinking of how to help this little family and walking those many miles with a coal bucket and curtains in the hopes that, in some small way, he could make their lives a bit more tolerable. He was always thinking of others.

"What did she do with them?"

Marie told us that her mother had sewed the curtains into baby bedding for her newborn cousin—and the baby was one of the women we had met today! A big grin came across Dad's face. All he wanted to know was that he had helped.

We talked all afternoon. "Anything I ever knew about French, you taught me," Dad said to Marie when we asked him how he learned his French.

"I wish you would have taught him better," I remarked to Marie with a giggle.

We continued our conversation at a lovely local restaurant. Remembering the nearly empty church we had attended on Sunday, I asked Christian and Beatrice why the churches are so empty now, when Europe had been the seat of Christendom. They simply replied, "It is not so popular now."

Dad and Marie sat beside each other, and we talked all evening. In spite of the language barrier, they were beaming and laughing like teenagers. We finally returned to the Hotel Amigo around 11:30. Dad mused out loud, "I wonder what life would have been like if I had stayed in Belgium. Maybe my French would have been better." And that was all he would say out loud about his musings and what-ifs.

WEDNESDAY, MARCH 9, 2005, VERVIERS, BELGIUM

I miss my family. But Dad is pumped to see everyone, especially Marie, of course. And being here is advancing my mission of learning more about him. Things just pop into his head over here, even though they have been lying dormant for sixty years. For example, he remembered this morning that Marie's maiden name when he first knew her was Klackenburg. He was also looking forward to meeting Jean-Claude Hendrick, a resident of a small village called Stavelot, who erected a memorial to the twelve American soldiers and three citizens

of Stavelot who were murdered in a massacre by the Nazis during the
Battle of the Bulge.

When I asked what the difference was between a murder and a regular kill in combat (after all, the end result is the same), Dad explained.
The Third Geneva Convention of 1929, to which the Germans were sig-
natories, made it illegal to torture or otherwise mistreat prisoners of war.
Instead of taking them as POWs, they were killed execution-style, not in
combat, which I suppose would have been a "fair kill." But I don't know
the whole story or the rules of engagement for when killing is considered
"fair." It all seems horrific to me.

At any rate, Beatrice and Marie picked us up in the afternoon, and
we drove to Stavelot to see Jean-Claude and his monument. He was
delighted to greet a member of "The Phantom Nine," as he called the
9th Armored Division, and he came outside to greet us as we pulled into
the driveway of his home. His house was modest, and a wood-burning
stove in the living room provided the only heat. The house was full of
antiques of humble origin and stacks of books and knickknacks. Cob-
webs hung from the high ceilings. A large handmade sign proclaimed,
"Welcome Mr. Richard Quint, 27th Infantry Bn., 9th Armored Division." An American flag hung on the left side of the sign, and a Belgian
flag was on the right. Before we even sat down, he showed us with great
pride a plaque presented to him by the 9th Armored Division for his
"friendship and special recognition."

We looked through a number of old pictures. Dad presented him
with a picture book of the United States, and he presented Dad with
a bit of the Belgian flag ribbon that was used during the commemoration ceremony of his memorial in 1987. The best I could understand
the story (from the little French I could make out—which was at least
better than my German) was that forty years after witnessing the massacre, Jean-Claude had felt compelled to honor the fallen soldiers. He had

contacted the director of the technical and trade school that he attended and asked if he could use the school's facilities to forge the bronze plaque for the monument. In exchange, he offered to let the school official use his vacation home in the mountains. The plaque was forged and put on a large stone. A number of American military representatives, including a retired general, a colonel, and several soldiers (both active and retired), plus local officials attended the commemoration ceremony in 1987.

We trudged through the snow outside the village to the hill on which the monument stood. It was overcast and damp, and halfway up the hill, a rain and snow mixture started falling. It seemed appropriately somber weather to visit a memorial. Jean-Claude carried an American flag given to him by Robert Patterson of the 9th Armored Division. (I don't know if he was any relation to our Iva Rose Patterson). The flag had flown over the capitol in Washington, DC. Jean-Claude was quite proud of the flag, the monument he had built, and his long-distance friendship with the U.S. and the 9th Armored Division.

When we arrived at the monument, I was surprised at how big it was—at least seven feet high and just as wide. We read aloud each name of the fallen soldiers whose murders Jean-Claude had witnessed as a young boy and offered a silent prayer. Jean-Claude and Dad ceremoniously held the flag up by the monument. Then Dad showed him the proper way to fold it. Tears welled up in Beatrice's eyes at our mini-ceremony to honor these fallen soldiers who had given their lives for a country that wasn't their own so that Belgium could be free. There were tears in mine too.

We trudged back through the snow, down the hill, and to the village where Jean-Claude showed us several monuments, many of which honored the Americans who had fought. One monument was in memory of the 138 civilians who were killed. The names on the plaque indicated that entire families were wiped out during the Nazi invasion at what is now known as the Battle of the Bulge. There were also memorials to the

Belgian soldiers of WWI. This poor little peaceful hamlet had seen too many wars, too much bloodshed.

We walked up to a large white building with wood beams, the same building I had seen in advertising brochures enticing people to come to "charming Stavelot."

"This is the building my unit stayed in in December of '44," Dad said.

"What did your unit do?"

"Well, the whole unit was a noncombat unit."

"Noncombat. What does that mean? Didn't you fight? Didn't you have guns?"

"No, I was a medic."

Dad had been transferred to a combat unit by the time he had reached the Remagen bridge, but now I was hearing that, until then, he was a medic. But of course—that's so much like Dad. He loves helping people. He hates to see anyone get hurt. At least the army had him pegged right.

"On December 16 of '44," Dad continued, "my commanding officer told our unit that we should be ready to leave at a moment's notice. About midnight, we got orders to leave because the Germans were coming over that hill." He pointed up the hill. The same hill where the soldiers were killed and on which Jean-Claude's monument now stands. The same hill we had just walked down. I looked up the road we had just come down—it was less than a mile from the building we were standing by. If they had not left immediately, as a noncombat unit they would have shared the same fate as the murdered soldiers. I contemplated for a moment how close Dad and his unit had come to being killed, and how close I came to never existing. This seemed to be a whole trip filled with wonderings, of what-ifs. The dates on the memorials were December 17, 18, and 19, 1944. Clearly, Dad's name could have been on one of the memorials. But I guess it was not his time.

Jean-Claude was having a great time showing us the memorials around town and the half-track (which had the names of all the units stationed there at one time or another during World War II, including Dad's 96th Replacement Battalion), and the house of some general. He seemed completely oblivious to the cold and was relishing his duties as self-appointed tour guide. But we were freezing in the snow and rain. We finally made our way back to Jean-Claude's house, where his wife and Marie had coffee and muffins waiting for us. I warmed my now frozen wet feet by their wood-burning stove and sat back to listen to the half-French, half-American chatter of the afternoon.

Before we left, I pulled out an angel pin that I had brought with me from the States and presented it to Jean-Claude. "Thank you for your friendship. This little angel pin symbolizes my wish that angels will watch over you and keep you safe." Beatrice, as she had done all day, translated for me. Jean-Claude immediately wanted me to put the pin on his sweater, which I did. He was beaming.

As we left, there were many hugs and thank-yous. Mme. Hendrick took Dad's hand in both of hers and expressed in heartfelt, though broken, English, "Thank you for your service and what you did for our country."

Dad, in his understated way, and not forgetting he almost hadn't made it out of Stavelot in '44, said, "I'm glad to be here to accept your thanks."

We returned to Marie's house in Verviers, where Marienne had made sandwiches for dinner. We were joined by yet another group of Marie's family. Marienne showed me an old photograph that she had found. It was a yellowed picture of my sister and me taken on Halloween. I looked ridiculous. It was one of those pictures I had hoped remained stuffed in the bottom of a drawer, but here was a copy in Belgium!

"Do you know this? Your sister sent it to me when we were pen pals."

I was a bit surprised at seeing a picture of myself half a world away—though perhaps I shouldn't have been. It was so like Dad to foster international relations and to want his girls to be friends with the daughters of his friends. He initiated the pen pal program between Marienne and my big sister, Kathy, when he was stationed in Europe in 1972.

"Of course I do. It's me and my sister at Halloween. I was about five, and she's about eight. Dad had made my costume that year out of chicken wire, orange crepe paper, and green construction paper—it was Charlie Brown's 'The Great Pumpkin,' and my sister has a stuffed Snoopy in her hands. All you can see of me are my legs poking out from under a giant orange pumpkin. He was so proud of the costume that I hardly got a chance to go trick or treating—he was too busy showing me off to his friends the whole night!"

We enjoyed an evening listening to stories of years past and looking through old photographs of Dad and Marie (but none of them together!). Dad presented Marie with a picture book of Chicago which he had inscribed inside the front cover. I had actually purchased a few of those picture books for gifts (suspecting that Dad, being a man, might forget about bringing presents for our hosts—which, of course, he did). At his age, Dad was having difficulty writing, so the message was short and sweet—and none of us but Marie knows what he wrote.

I presented Marie with one of my angel pins. "Thank you for being an angel to my dad and to our troops. I pray the angels will watch over you."

"*Merci,*" was her simple answer, with tears welling in her eyes.

As we were leaving, Dad burst into song as a final serenade to his dear friend, "Marie, the dawn is breaking. Marie, my heart is aching . . ." and then we were out the door, but not before extending a sincere invitation to Marie and her family to come visit us in the States. We knew it was unlikely that at her age Marie would ever make it across the pond. She stood on the doorstep and waved what she knew was her final goodbye to her Dick.

MARCH 10, 2005, THURSDAY ALTENBURG, GERMANY, 10 PM

"Love is patient, love is kind."

—1 CORINTHIANS 13:4

I started today wishing to be back home, and I was wishing it even more by the end of the day. This was the part of the trip I had tried to skip. I had tried to convince Dad that we could bypass this portion (in favor of maybe just *one* day of sightseeing in a town that *I* would be interested in seeing), but he would have none of it. He wanted to see people in the tiny town of Altenburg, which is all the way across Germany by the Czech border. I still have no idea why, as he only stayed in the town for two days and had no contact with these people for sixty years—because they ended up being part of East Germany after the war, contact was not really possible. On top of that, they only speak German. Further still, Altenburg takes several trains and twelve hours to get to!

But Dad was insistent. So we started at ten a.m. from Verviers and took four trains and rented a car, but only missed one major turn, and at ten p.m. have finally arrived in Altenburg—where no one speaks English. While Dad seemed fine upon arrival, my nerves were completely unraveled from doing all the planning, all the driving, all the navigation in a language I couldn't read, all the translation (I don't even speak German), and all the worrying about how to not miss the next train. The fact that the rental car I had reserved was not at the train station in Leipzig when we arrived, and that I missed a turn on a dark country road in the dead of night, frazzled my last remaining nerve. I just wanted a bed.

When we finally arrived at our hotel, I found that the double twin-bed room that I had reserved was not available (despite our being the only people in the hotel) and that the only clean room they had was one with a double bed. *Aaaarrrgghhhh!* Dad took one of the mattresses and slept on the floor. I nearly blew it when he insisted that we drive tomorrow morning to some place called Wintersdorf to see the barn that he once stayed in. I had no map and was not at all in the mood to get lost again. Dad was not at all aware of the massive effort I was putting forth and seemed completely impervious and uninterested in the toll that travel was taking on my nerves. I had not anticipated that traveling with my eighty-two-year-old father would be like traveling with my six-year-old son, except that Dad could be more demanding. I was exhausted and wallowing in self-pity.

On the bright side, however, while Hertz did not have anyone at the car rental desk when we arrived at 10 p.m. at the Bahnhauf in Leipzig, and while everyone at Hertz spoke only German or Russian (having been behind the Iron Curtain for fifty years), a wonderful person named Silvana who worked at the Sixt Car Rental next to it took pity on us, spoke English to us, and went out of her way to help us with a rental car. She even attempted to program the destination into the GPS system, although to no avail. *Mental note to self: next time in Germany, rent from Sixt, not Hertz; send Silvana a thank-you note.*

Earlier, we also chatted on the train with a wonderful young man named Sebastian, who made sure we were headed to the correct Altenburg, not Altenberg. (As it turned out, fortunately, the Altenburg I had identified and made reservations for was the correct one, but Dad mistakenly had the other one in mind.)

After a hot bath and two Tylenol PMs, I am finally going to bed, hoping that I will be in better spirits and more charitable to Dad in the morning. I hate being such a grump.

MARCH 11, 2005, FRIDAY, ON THE TRAIN FROM LEIPZIG TO ERLANGER
Breakfast today was very quiet. I was trying to figure out how to get to Wintersdorf, wherever that is, with no map and no one who could speak English to give me directions.

How in the world have we gone through the rest of Germany and found everyone to speak at least a little English, but we arrive in Leipzig and Altenburg and everyone speaks only German or Russian? Are they really incapable of a word of English, or are they just refusing to speak it? I hear from so many of my friends who visit Paris about the snobby French waiters who refuse to speak English to Americans. Are we getting the same treatment?

I was beginning to feel that the people in this region were quite inhospitable, only adding to my frustration. I was also trying to figure out how in the world we were going to communicate with these folks.

As I found out last night when I tried to telephone Dad's friends in Wintersdorf, they did not speak even one word of English, so I hauled out my German-English dictionary and we somehow managed to arrange a meeting at the hotel at which we were staying for ten this morning. I was already tired of doing all the translating while Dad relied on what little he learned sixty years ago. For reasons I do not know, he chose to speak German while in Belgium and French while in Germany. That way no one ever knew what he was talking about. Perhaps he thought it was funny, but I was not amused. And when he spoke in English, he (quite uncharacteristically) spoke in complex sentences and highbrow vocabulary—which most people found impossible to translate.

He is a simple man from a small town in downstate Illinois, so I was also beside myself in trying to figure out why he, all of a sudden, was speaking more like a college professor than good old Dad. Despite my admonitions to use simple words and sentences so people could translate more easily, he simply refused to do so—requiring me to translate his sentences into simple "Dick and Jane" plain English so our friends could figure out what he was saying. My frustration level was rising.

At any rate, the cook at the hotel spoke broken English, which he had learned as a sailor on an oil ship. Thankfully, he agreed to translate when our friends came, and he did his best, since we were the only ones in the hotel that night.

At ten a.m., Gelda, her husband, and her brother-in-law arrived. They were short and plain, and she had the short, curly grey hair that grandmas in their seventies wear. Dad had stayed in Gelda's house when she was a young woman during the war. Dad had told me that her sister, Linda, was beautiful. We sat down at the table for coffee. Our hosts told us that Gelda's husband (then her boyfriend) was a German soldier during World War II and fought in Russia. They married after the war, and he became an elementary school teacher and then a principal.

Who would have imagined a World War II German soldier and a World War II American solder having coffee together after all of these years? Leave it to Dad to come halfway across the world to mend fences over a cup of coffee!

Then something extraordinary happened. Dad reminded Gelda that when he left, her mother had told him that she had a brother in Chicago. She had written down his name, address, and phone number and asked my dad to contact him when returned stateside. Even though Dad was a Minnesota boy at the time, he had kept his promise to find him.

"Well, I telephoned, but he didn't believe me at first. So I took a bus to Chicago to find him. Then I went to his house and showed him the paper with your mom's handwriting. I guess he finally believed me then and talked to me. He's a butcher, you know." As if reporting back on the status of a mission impossible, Dad reported to Gelda that he had kept his promise to her mother.

Dad had, miraculously, kept that piece of paper in his wallet for the last sixty years. He slowly pulled it out.

"I had it laminated last year. It was falling apart," he said apologetically as he gave it to Gelda, as if presenting her with a gold treasure.

At that moment, I finally began to understand why we came here. *Dad is going on his farewell tour in the twilight of his life. He wants to*

*reconnect with all the people in his life who made a difference—who
touched him, who were kind to him. He wants to tell them that he kept his
promises—that their trust in him was not misplaced and that their kindness was not wasted. And he even wants to reconnect them to relatives
who have lost touch and perhaps lost their way because of the war. While
I have been whining about not being able to see the great sights of Europe
and getting lost and staying in C-grade hotels, Dad has never lost sight of
the important things in life—and indeed, of our very reason for coming.
He has always valued relationships over everything else—money, power,
fame, everything. And our visit is not about seeing the great architecture
or historical sights of Europe. It is his last effort to restore his relationships and let them know that he treasures them.*

How could I have been so blind and selfish? My grumpiness and icy
disposition melted in the warmth of such kindness.

Gelda immediately recognized the handwriting of her mother,
who had long since passed away. "*Danke schoen*," she whispered softly
through her tears.

Mission accomplished.

*"The measure of a man's real character is what he would do if
he knew he would never be found out."*

—THOMAS BABINGTON MACAULAY

Gelda's brother-in-law offered to drive us to Wintersdorf to see her
sister, who was living in the house where my dad had stayed while he
was stationed there. Dad took all of a second to accept the invitation
(knowing that I wouldn't drive), and we were off just like that.

I saw the countryside in the daylight for the first time. Wintersdorf
was a small village of several hundred people. There were many dilapidated
houses on the way there and several that appeared to have been bombed

(maybe as long ago as the war) and simply abandoned. It was nothing like the rest of the beautiful Germany that I had seen with neat white houses with orange roofs, all well-kept and tidy. I soon found out why.

We met Gelda's sister, Linda, and her grandson in Wintersdorf. Her grandson (thankfully) spoke English and had just graduated from college. Although he lived in another town, he came to translate and perhaps get a history lesson. We settled in to Linda's tiny living room, which was about as big as my bathroom. They explained that when the Americans left after World War II, the Russians took over, and they were under Communist rule until the fall of the Berlin Wall. Before today, I had never met any East Germans who had lived under Communism—and my curiosity got the better of me.

"So what differences have you noticed living under Communism as compared to after the fall of the Berlin Wall?" I tried to put my question as delicately as I could.

"Well, back then, luxuries like television were enormously expensive," Linda's grandson responded. *Did he just say a television was a luxury?*

He continued, "It took ten years for a phone line to be installed." *Did I hear him right? Ten years for a phone? Good gracious!*

"There were never any new homes or building construction because the raw materials were too difficult to find and too expensive." *I guess that explains the dilapidated buildings. But, geez, it's been sixteen years since the fall of Communism. Doesn't anyone fix things up? Let's get a move on!*

"The waiting list for a new car, Russian-made of course, was eighteen years. And you had to sign up on a list to get one. But you couldn't sign up on the list until you were eighteen years old. So the earliest you could get a new car was when you turned thirty-six." *You have got to be kidding!*

"A new TV took about ten years on the waiting list." *So much for the MTV generation. They completely missed it.*

"And English was never taught in school. Only German and Russian." *Well, that explains why no one in this region will talk to me. I guess they aren't rude and inhospitable after all.*

"So the transition to one Germany wasn't easy. Many people were unemployed. At least under Communism there was job security. I am the first in my family to get a college degree in business, and I am still looking for a job." *Well, if any of those liberal socialists back home have a problem with capitalism, we should ship them right over here to see how things work without it.*

Enough about politics—Dad wanted to see the house and the building where a number of displaced persons from Eastern Europe were staying at the time he was stationed there. So we took a little tour through town. The building he remembered was still there. It had been an old cow barn. *We don't have time to see Brussels or Brugge or Bach's museum in Leipzig or Martin Luther's church because you had to spend two days to travel to see a cow barn? Ah well, there will be plenty of opportunities in my lifetime to see the sights of Europe. Today . . . Dad and I need to see a cow barn.*

Before we left the house, Dad had to sing one more song to Linda, the gal he had once thought was so beautiful. "I used to sing it to you back in '45, but you didn't know the words in English, so you always stomped your foot at me and told me to stop," he reminisced with a twinkle in his eye. Dad's baritone voice was sweet and smooth as he crooned to "Somewhere Over the Rainbow." This time Linda didn't stomp her foot.

We made it back to the hotel and had to decline a lovely invitation to lunch so that we could drive back to Leipzig and catch our train on time. I tried to drop the car off at the car rental place at the Leipzig train station, but with all the traffic and crazy one-way streets, I ended up across the street and unable to get there. So I abandoned the rental car in front of the Holiday Inn and went into the train station to plead for mercy so that someone from the car rental counter would take pity on us and retrieve the car for me. Fortunately, our angel Silvana was working again and happily came out to help us. After she rescued us (again), we gave her a generous tip, and I made a mental note to write to Sixt Car Rental and give her a commendation.

We grabbed lunch and souvenirs in the Leipzig train station before heading off to Nuremberg. I am looking forward to seeing our good friends the Blank family in cute little Schlaifhausen. But now, a little nap on the train.

"Kindness is the language which the deaf can hear and the blind can see."

—MARK TWAIN

REMINISCING ABOUT DAD

SOMETIME IN 1995

Dad was always befriending those young men who needed a dad, either because theirs had died or because theirs were not interested in being dads. In the sixties, one young airman, Gary Ingle, lived in the trailer next door to our house. He had a small civil wedding with Maggie, and Mom and Dad hosted a modest reception at our house. The most I remember about Gary in those days is that he had a pet skunk and that it pooped on my leg when I was five. Gary is in his sixties now and is an engineer and a grandpa. He and Dad go fishing every year in Minnesota. He always reminds me of the days living in the trailer next to our house, when he was young and wild and rode motorcycles. Dad was his instructor at Chanute Air Force Base, mentor, surrogate dad, and friend.

Another young friend was Bruce Vetter, whose father, Clyde, was my dad's good friend. Clyde was a man's man— he flew B-24s in the war and ate nails for breakfast—but he was not much of a family man. Dad took Bruce, the youngest, under his wing as Bruce was growing up and into motorcycles and long hair and other cultural phenomena of the 1970s. The friendship has continued ever since, and Dad fills in as grandpa for Bruce's kids.

"You know, Dick, you are more of a father than my own father is. My dad has never told me that he loves me—ever."

"I know, Bruce. I don't know why he can't say that. But I know your dad loves you. I love you too, you know."

"I know, Dick. I love you too."

Saturday, March 12, 2005 Schlaifhausen, Germany

"Are not all angels ministering spirits sent to help and care for us?"

—Hebrews 1:14 (paraphrased)

When we arrived in the Erlangen train station last night, we were greeted by Klothilda and her daughter Daniela. It was good to see familiar faces and to get a heartfelt bear hug. Daniela's birthday was March 7, but she delayed her birthday party so that we could join in the celebration.

As we were descending the steps at the station, I asked Dad if I could take his bag. It was at the most twenty pounds, but he was not as strong as he used to be, and he was dragging it step by step either up or down the stairs, wherever we went. Most of the old train stations had no elevators or escalators, and it was survival of the fittest up and down the steps. I had asked several times before on the trip, but he always brushed me off—"I can do it! Let me do *something!*" I had obviously struck a sensitive chord and had, in my efforts to help, been inadvertently insensitive to an older man who realized that he was losing his strength and masculinity and was trying to hold on to the manhood he had left. *As someone who was once a soldier and worked with his hands his whole life, it must be frustrating to get old and lose the ability to do the things he is used to doing.*

He refused to let me take his bag, so I started down the steps with my own (which must have been close to sixty or seventy pounds), intending to drop it off at the bottom and come back to get Dad's. I never got the chance. I heard a big commotion behind me, and as I looked back, I saw Dad sliding down the stairs surrounded by people. One foot was several steps above the rest of his body, and his leg was contorted in a position that only gymnasts should ever be in. I hurried back up, and we slowly helped him get both his feet under himself. He had slipped with his bag, but of course he blamed it on "those dadgum plastic-soled shoes!" A very nice young man helped him down the steps—and I, of course, carried his bag like I should have in the first place.

"Let me call a doctor for you," the thoughtful young man said in a thick German accent.

"No, no. I don't need a darn doctor!" Dad wouldn't hear of it.

We thanked the gentleman profusely, and when he realized that my dad was adamant about not seeing a doctor, he finally went on his way. Daniela pulled her car up the sidewalk all the way to the bottom of the steps. We stuffed suitcases and people into the tiny European car, and we were off.

When we arrived at Klothilda's house in Schlaifhausen, Daniela's party was already in progress. The Germans certainly know how to throw a party, and the tiny house was overflowing with people. Klothilda's nephew, Horst, and her son-in-law, Didi, helped Dad in, and we plopped him on a chair with strict orders not to move. The beer was flowing freely, and the festive mood livened Dad's spirits.

I distributed the gifts I had brought, happy to get some weight out of my bags. Since Daniela is a baker, I gave her an Illinois cookbook, along with measuring cups and teaspoons. As I had learned on our last trip, German recipes call for grams and kilograms, not teaspoons and cups, and I wanted to make sure she had all the necessary equipment for U.S. recipes. For Klothilda, I had quilted a table runner. For Horst, a banker, I brought cufflinks; for Klothilda's husband, Walter, a cashmere scarf; Chicago Bears hats for the men and boys; freshwater pearl necklaces and Marshall Field's bags and purses for the little girls, Klothilda's grandchildren; and a picture book of Illinois for Klothilda and Walter.

No matter what culture we are from, everyone hopes to give gifts that are appreciated. I am no exception. The Blanks are hardworking and of modest means, and I hoped these would be special treats. I wasn't disappointed. Either the gifts were a big hit, or they were extremely gracious. Klothilda assured me that we had overdone our gift-giving, and just like my mother would do, promptly put the quilted table cover in the living room so that no one would spill anything on it. Daniela was excited to get started on cooking and was both perplexed and delighted by the names of our favorite Midwestern dishes, like "seven-layer bars," "chili" (which is usually anything but), and "pigs in a blanket." Walter, usually very quiet (the exact opposite of Klothilda) simply said "Danke," and flamboyant Horst was thrilled with his new fashion statement. Laura, Klothilda's granddaughter, immediately took off her necklace and assured me that she would wear the pearls for her first communion, which was that upcoming Sunday. It seemed very appropriate, since Dad's connection with this family came from Klothilda's first communion, that we somehow were connected to her granddaughter's.

Klothilda brought out her scrapbook from her trip to Illinois in 2000. It was obviously the biggest trip of her life, and her only one to the States. Mom and Dad had kept her very busy. Along with pictures from Springfield, Lincoln's home, and visits to farms in downstate Illinois, there were also pictures from her visit to us in Chicago. There were even pictures of my house and my bathroom! Clearly, our houses in the U.S. were on a larger scale than those she was used to, and she wanted to show everyone at home how we lived in America. We all had a big laugh, especially over the bathroom photo.

Tilda and Dad quickly turned to reminiscing about how they had first met. We were all eager to hear more of their stories, which seemed to come out in bits and pieces each time they were together. They picked up the conversation from where we left off last year, without missing a beat. Through Daniela, our translator, Tilda reminded us, "When the American soldiers first came, the children were afraid of them. But the soldiers gave us our first chocolate bars! It was in a brown wrapper and covered in silver foil."

"It was a Hershey's bar," Dad piped in.

"The Americans gave us hot lunches at school. Soon we got over our fear."

Each time the story is told, we get more details. We settled in for a long story.

"On the day Richard shot the photograph of us, all the girls were afraid of him, except for me."

"Mom was the littlest and feistiest of them all," Daniela explained.

"All the girls wore white flowers in their headbands. So to make us unafraid of him, Richard put a white handkerchief on his head and started dancing around like a clown. We couldn't be afraid of someone who was dancing around like a fool with a handkerchief on his head, even if he was a soldier. So we let him take a picture of us."

We all burst into laughter at the thought of Dad dancing around with a handkerchief on his head. It reminded me of so many times when we were growing up when he would put on a ridiculous hat and dance around like he had just escaped from the psych ward. He was especially fond of putting the earflaps on his old leather flight helmet out and letting them flop up and down like a duck trying to take flight as he waved his arms up and down. Then he would slide his glasses down his nose and cross his eyes. I was always perplexed as to whether he did this just to embarrass me or because he liked to be goofy. Maybe a little bit of both. In any event, my friends loved him, so I didn't mind being embarrassed.

We insisted that Dad put on a handkerchief and reenact the scene. Always pleased to be part of the party, he happily obliged. Thankfully, Tilda had an extra pair of crutches, and Dad was back in business. With his crutches and arms flailing, a white handkerchief on his head, and a dance resembling the chicken dance, we laughed until tears came to our eyes at the silly sight.

After a few beers made at a local brewery by one of the Blank relatives and homemade hooch and cheers to "Miss Sophie"—a German version of a *Saturday Night Live* skit played every New Year's Eve—we finally turned in around midnight.

This morning we had a leisurely late breakfast which Dad followed with a nap. Then we squeezed into Horst's little car, complete with a Pink Floyd customization that I have never seen in the States, to take a tour of Ebermannstadt, a neighboring town to Schlaifhausen. Our first stop was the church where Dad had first taken the photo of Klothilda and her girlfriends on the day of their first communion. The date of that encounter always seemed to change from story to story—I had heard Corpus Christi Day, Ascension Day, and first communion. So today we finally got the date cleared up—it was not only the day of their first communion but also Corpus Christi Day, which is also very close to Ascension Day. So everyone was right. At any rate, it was sometime in late May, 1945.

The church was a modest Roman Catholic one made of stucco, stone, and wood, tucked among the cobblestone streets of the village. It had ancient oak pews, stained-glass windows, and a stone floor that echoed even the slightest sound.

"This is the pew that I always sat in," Klothilda explained through her translator Daniela, pointing to the third pew on the left. "Since I was so little, I always had to sit with my aunt close to the front." I wondered if she had to sit so close to the front because of her feistiness too.

Next, we visited the tiny little chapel where Klothilda and Walter were married. Dad remembered the little stream that ran through town and recalled playing pickup games of football in the field by the stream. "Yeah, I had to dive in and fish a guy out of the river because he fell in and couldn't swim," he recalled nonchalantly. He had never even mentioned it before. So typical, heroes don't think that their heroic acts—like saving someone's life—are heroic.

We met up with Regina and Christina, two more of the "little girls" from the first communion picture, at a local coffeehouse. Although I like European coffee, the "bottomless cup," or even one free refill is, unfortunately, a uniquely American concept. It was another wonderful reunion. The girls had a good laugh as Horst reminded them of the handkerchief that my dad had danced around in. Regina also reminded them of their first taste of chocolate from the American GIs. Although chocolate might be a small, unremarkable thing to us, it was obviously quite memorable for these ladies, who reminded us each time we were together. Sadly, remembering the silly antics of my dad also brought out hurtful memories of the war. Each in turn told us how her father had been forced to fight for the Nazi army and sent to fight on the Russian front. Even after so many years, the emotions seemed to surface like it was yesterday.

Then Tilda shared the sweetest story. "After Walter and I were married, we had five girls. But my best friend died with small children, and then my sister died with small children. So Walter and I took in all the children, and we raised all ten together in our house in Schlaifhausen." *Twelve people in that little house! Goodness!*

"What did Walter do?" I asked.

"He was a bricklayer."

"Ten children on a bricklayer's salary! You were busy!" *Wow. She really* is *an angel.*

"Mama was the general!" Daniela piped in with a smile, playfully saluting the general.

"We were very busy raising so many kids. But when I met your mom and dad together, they called each other 'honey' and 'sweetheart'—and they were in their seventies! I was so busy raising kids, I just called Walter 'Walter.' Not honey or sweetheart. But it is good to do that. Your mom and dad showed me that."

We returned to Tilda's house for lunch, which was the most delicious pork roast I had ever tasted. Knowing that this was probably Dad's last trip to Germany, and knowing his love for these "angels" he had found in Ebermannstadt so many years ago, I had brought some gifts to reflect their angel connection.

"In remembrance of the church and your first communion on the day that you first met my dad," I said as I gave each of them a cross necklace. "And because Dad always calls you his 'Angels of Ebermannstadt,' this is for the angels to always watch over you," I said as I gave each of them an angel pin. It was very quiet—I could hear only the sniffles of Klothilda as she put on her necklace and I helped her with her pin.

Regina gave me another pair of beautiful hand-knit socks, "In remembrance of when Dick and the other soldiers would give their gloves to the children of Ebermannstadt so that their mothers could use the yarn to knit sweaters and clothes," Daniela translated. I received a pair to give to Mom when I returned. Christy and Marty also received hand-knit chicks for Easter. Christina (who couldn't knit with only one arm) gave us Easter candy for the children and bottles of German wine for Dad and me. Tilda gave us Easter goodies for the children and lovely Easter table runners for Mom and me.

Dad and Regina and Christina knew that this would be their last good-bye—at least this side of heaven. The hugs were long. No one even attempted to hold back tears.

Dad has made one final checkup on his beloved Angels of Ebermannstadt and found all to be in order. He can go now.

Maybe he didn't change the world. But what he did sixty years ago, and what he does every day of his life, well, he sure changed his little corner of it. And Klothilda—look at the lives she changed by opening her heart and home to five orphans. And look at the lives they touched, and on and on. The ripple effects are endless. If we only say "Yes, Lord, use me. Use my hands and use my feet to love others," what amazing things we could accomplish!

"There are three kinds of people in the world today. There are 'well poisoners,' who discourage you and stomp on your creativity and tell you what you can't do. There are 'lawn-mowers,' people who are well-intentioned but self-absorbed; they tend to their own needs, mow their own lawns, and never leave their yards to help another person. Finally, there are 'life-enhancers,' people who reach out to enrich the lives of others, to lift them up and inspire them. We need to be life-enhancers, and we need to surround ourselves with life-enhancers."

—WALT DISNEY[2]

2 Quoted in John C. Maxwell, *Encouragement Changes Everything: Bless and Be Blessed* (Nashville, TN: Thomas Nelson, 2008), 19.

Sunday, March 13, 2005, on the Plane from Munich to Chicago

Dad and I set off, crutches and all, to the train station for Munich last evening to catch our plane home today. But before we left, we extracted a promise from Daniela and Tilda to visit us in the States soon.

The train personnel were very accommodating and helped us with our luggage. They even had a golf cart waiting to pick us up at the Munich train station. We hopped a cab to our hotel, which was just a block away. We actually stayed in the same room that Dad and Marty stayed in last year. After about forty-five minutes of phone calls, I finally was able to get through to the proper airline people to order a wheelchair in the airports. Then I ordered room service—sausages, of course—and crashed.

We had a very early start to the day—a wakeup call at 3:30 a.m. *Ouch!* Our taxi came at 4:15, and we arrived at the airport at five for a 7:15 flight. With a bit of effort, we finally procured wheelchairs and made it through the Munich, Heathrow, and O'Hare airports.

My mind was a cacophony of thoughts as we flew across the ocean that separated home from the lands which have had so much impact on my father's life.

Dad's life has come full circle. What he set out to do as a young man of seventeen, he accomplished—and he had the privilege to review his work as an older man of eighty-two. Like so many others, he put duty, honor, and country over his own personal ambitions and safety. He entered a living hell to fight for a land that was not his own, to give freedom to people he would never see. He saw comrades die beside him in battle and witnessed unspeakable cruelty. But through the darkness, this simple man of faith allowed God to use him, even in the midst of war, to be the light that God calls us to be. And in His grace, God allowed him to find people in the darkness who were shining their lights as well.

I think God puts people in our paths for His purposes, so that each of us, as ordinary as we may be, can have the privilege of being His hands and feet in that moment— if we only will let Him use us, if we only will see others through God's eyes. The people who crossed Dad's path during his life, and those who were in his path on these trips, were no accident. Dad extended the hand of friendship and the grace of forgiveness to German soldiers who desperately needed forgiveness and wanted someone to understand their impossible choice of fighting for the Nazis or allowing themselves and their families to be slaughtered; he kept a promise to a woman he would never see again and reported that he had been a worthy recipient of her trust to her daughter; he honored and bid good-bye to a dear friend who, perhaps under different times and circumstances, might have been something much more; he encouraged men and women who tirelessly work toward peace and friendship; he gave guidance and wisdom to active troops wrestling with some of life's most haunting questions; he surveyed and was pleased with the success of the lands he had helped liberate; and, like a kindly and protective older brother, he made one last check-in to make sure the flame of faith and friendship would ever shine bright in the hearts of his beloved Angels of Ebermannstadt.

Mission accomplished.

POSTLUDE

We came home to find that Mom had suffered a stroke while we were gone—although she did not know at the time what it was. It left her with difficulty speaking and writing and finding words. A trip to the doctor (as soon as she would let me take her) confirmed that it had been a ministroke in a series of ministrokes. I had hoped to take her to the opening of the Japanese-American museum in Los Angeles where they were honoring the courageous women, like Mom and her best friend Charlene Pease, who taught school at the Japanese internment camps during World War II. It was not to be.

Klothilda and Daniela did come and visit us in September of 2005. They even came to Christy's fifth-grade class with my dad, and they told of their experiences to a captivated audience of eleven-year-olds. The children's eyes were as big as quarters, and they were enthralled to have their history books come to life. They came from many different backgrounds—Christian, Jewish, Muslim, German, Greek, Italian—and they asked countless questions. With all of their freedoms, these children had a hard time understanding why the Germans of Klothilda's day were not even allowed to say "Good morning" instead of "Heil Hitler." They wanted to know why the Germans persecuted the Jews, they wanted to know why the whole country followed Hitler, and they wanted to know why the Germans thought the Aryan race should rule the world. It was all Klothilda could do to answer them all without

sobbing. But she knew, like I knew and Dad knew, that the next generation needed to know the story so that it would never happen again. I
handed her a tissue to wipe away the tears. "Danke."

In the end, Klothilda reminded the class—and me—of that universal truth that we all know, but somehow manage to forget from time to
time with all the busyness of our lives. "Going through life, and especially during those difficult days," she said, "it is good to have a friend.
And Dick was my friend."

"Of all the good gifts that God gives us, perhaps no gift is
sweeter that the gift of friendship."

—CHARLENE QUINT KALEBIC

St. Francis of Assisi is credited with saying, "Preach the gospel at all
times. If necessary, use words." Without using words, Dad has spread
the gospel of peace on earth and goodwill toward men every day of
his life with his simple acts of friendship and kindness. While he has
never been one to evangelize about religion, he has spent his whole life
quietly trying to be more like Jesus in small ways—never preaching,
never judging, just doing. During the war, it was giving food and Hershey's chocolate bars to children, offering his gloves to make sweaters,
or making a ten-mile trek with a coal bucket and window curtains so
a mother could keep her children warm and make clothing for them.

He is always shoveling the neighbors' walks, mowing their lawns,
fixing things for people when they are sick (and when they aren't), welcoming his air force base students over to our house for Sunday pot
roast, being a father figure to kids who have none, being a father and
grandfather who offers unwavering support to his family, and simply
being a friend. Most recently, he single-handedly organized a drive
in his small town to collect toys and stuffed animals to send to Iraqi

children. He still remembers that everyone, especially children in war, need a friend.

Dad has two favorite verses that he shared with us. One is from Proverbs: "Trust in the Lord with all your heart and lean not upon your own understanding; in all your ways acknowledge him, and he will make your paths straight" (Proverbs 3:5–6). The other is from Romans: "And we know that in all things God works for the good of those who love him, who have been called according to his purpose" (Romans 8:28). God's promises in those two little verses got him through the war and got him through life.

As I write this at the age of forty-three, my life is more than half-lived, while Dad is entering his sunset years. I can't help but wonder what legacy I will leave. And I can't help but compare it to Dad's and to the people like him who, not unlike the angels, have loved by giving of themselves, oftentimes to strangers, and have made this world a little bit kinder and a little bit more like heaven. Will I be remembered by people whose lives have crossed my path for my acts of kindness, or have I been too busy to even notice them, much less take the time to help or encourage them? Would I really walk ten miles in the winter with a bucket of coal and window curtains to help another family, or would I just tell myself that it's too much effort and retreat to my comfortable, warm home? Would I have the courage to stand for justice, or would I be like those Germans who did nothing while a madman took control of their country? When my time on earth is over and God shows me the videotape of my life, will I be proud of the lives that were changed because of me, or ashamed because I was too engaged in achieving financial success to bother? Forty years hence, will I be able to survey the fruits of my labor in the form of successful lives in whom I have invested, or will I have invested only in stocks and bonds?

I have, perhaps, if I am fortunate, another forty-three years. And I feel that I had better make up for lost time.

GOING HOME

My dad went to be with his Lord on March 25, 2008, after a long battle with prostate cancer. When he was first diagnosed in February of 1998, I made an entry in my prayer journal. I asked God for ten more years with him—and if I got ten more years, I promised the Lord that I would not ask for more. The Lord gave me ten years and thirty-five days. I know it was a wonderful homecoming, as God welcomed him with the words we all long to hear: "Well done, good and faithful servant. Welcome home."

His kindness and humor and thoughtfulness of others remained to the end of his days. On our last day with him, with all of us snuggled up next to him on his bed, he could barely talk, but he managed a smile and affirmed, "It's wonderful to have a big family." And when I told him that I had seen his physician, Dr. Amesbury, that morning, rather than inquiring about his own condition, he beamed, "She's a delightful person, isn't she?"

Not only did he teach us how to live, he taught us how to die.

Friends and family remembered him with these remarks.

Remembering Dick Quint
by Kelly Vetter

I was speaking to the man who directs this funeral home yesterday, and he was talking about how Dick was a social gardener. That is so true. He'd get his basket of juicy ripe tomatoes, and like a circuit-riding preacher, make his rounds to neighbors and friends bringing good veggies and good company. He'd do the same in the fall with his basket of apples. I know because I could count on Dick to make us one of his stops. How glad we were.

I know Dick has been a friend to this family long before I came onto the scene. I can only speak to that which I witnessed. When he came through our doorway he always stretched out his arms for a hug and then handed out a compliment as if it were a prized jewel: "You're beautiful!," "Bruce has all the pretty girls in Homer," "I came just for that hug." He was always a gentleman.

I must tell one story on Dick that really got to Bruce. One visit, Dick was making his way up the stairs to Bruce's office. About halfway up, Bruce jumped up to get something to show Dick. As he was passing him, he cautioned Dick to go slow up the stairs, sit down, and wait for him. Bruce reminded Dick there was no railing on the stairs, to be careful, he didn't want him to fall. Bruce was and is a real stickler for safety. Upon Bruce's return he found the door shut to the landing and went to open it, but something was pressing against it, something unmistakably like a body. That was when Dick starting groaning. At first Bruce was horrified—*How could this happen?* Then he saw that sheepish grin come across Dick's face. Bruce didn't know whether to hug him with relief or kick him down the rest of the stairs. Dick was some jokester.

I must share that we have coined a phrase in our household and have used it for some time, that one should be, "Quint-like," meaning always taking the higher road in kindness, thoughtfulness, and honesty.

I end with this, for the best news I have today is knowing our good and kind friend was a believer. He didn't have to preach it, he just always walked it. So he drew all men unto Christ as the Lord said would happen if we live out our faith. And God set eternity in all our hearts; that is why this world will never bring true satisfaction, for we long for a home where no more tears are shed. And when I get there I want my mansion (for Jesus said He was going to prepare a place for us, and His Father's house has many mansions), well I want mine right next to Dick and Jean, so I can still get those hugs. But then I'll get them every morning instead of just on visits.

Remembering Dick Quint
by Kate Vetter Boyer

Dick has been a friend of my grandfather, Clyde, for about fifty years. Many of my memories are of them together, because at every visit, the Quints and the Surridges were always included with our family dinners.

When my grandmother passed away fifteen years ago, it seemed to us that every good thing in my grandfather passed away with her. He had very little contact with our family and wanted nothing to do with us. Dick, being such a kindhearted soul, was pained deeply. He made it his personal mission to change my grandfather's heart toward us. I am told that Dick wrote Clyde letters, visited him, and reminded him at every phone call that he was missing out on our lives. Without much progress being made, he took it upon himself to stand in where Clyde was no longer able to stand—as a loving grandfather to my family. The importance of this became clear to me about ten years ago when Rob and I started talking about marriage, and the sorrow and grief of my grandparents missing my whole adult life and the lives of my future children were overwhelming. I spent a day at the Quints' house, weeping on Jean's shoulder, grieving this loss. Jean and Dick comforted me with precious memories of my grandparents and helped me learn to let go.

The Quints have been wonderful grandparents. They have participated in every major event in my life and in the lives of my children. Dick and Jean's presence has enriched every birthday party, barbeque, and many "just a good day for a drive" visits. They have filled the void my grandparents left, beautifully. I could never have asked for better family.

And in God's incredible providence, a life lived well has impact even when it is over here on earth. About a month ago, my grandfather called me out of the blue. He told me that he's heard good things about me. He shared many memories that he had about Dick and inquired as to Dick's condition. In the end, he wanted to talk to me on a weekly basis—he tells me that he loves me, which I have never heard before. Every week that I talk to him, he shares kind things that I never knew he felt. We have begun a friendship that I never had any hope of having after my grandmother's passing. I know that Dick's influence and the Lord's softening of Clyde's heart is the only reason that I have been able to get to know my grandfather after all these years.

People always say the best things of you at your funeral—but I'm not going to wait that long. Jean is one of the most incredible women I have ever had the privilege of meeting. She embodies what it means to have a "quiet and gentle spirit." If I can "grow up" to be just a fraction of the woman that she is, I will consider myself exceedingly blessed. She will always be remembered and honored in our house every time we look at her namesake, my little Elizabeth Jean, and remind people (even strangers) that she is named after a very wise and loving family friend.

MR. QUINT: A REMEMBRANCE

by Michael Owens

As I've reflected on my memories of my friend Mr. Quint—he will always be "Mr. Quint" to me because our friendship dates back more than twenty years to when I was a sophomore at Rantoul Township High School, and no matter my middle-aged status today, somehow, in the context of my friendship with Mr. Quint, a part of me still feels like a teenager and I must therefore show him respect by not referring to him as "Dick"—and remembered him in e-mail communications with my dear friend Charlie, his youngest daughter, I'm reminded of what I'd call the "essential" Mr. Quint. He was a man with a genuine interest in and compassion for others, evidenced by his willingness to share with his friends and family himself, his resources, his humor, his time, and his abundant energy and enthusiasm.

The Quints first invited me into their home as their daughter's friend. Very quickly it was clear that any friend of Charlie's was as much a friend of theirs. It was important to Mr. Quint to be engaged in Charlie's life by knowing her activities and the friends she shared her time with. A (very lucky!) few of us remember his generosity of spirit one winter in the early 1980s when he invited us to drive to Wisconsin for a ski adventure. We piled into one of Mr. Quint's famous Suburbans and embarked on a whirlwind weekend that included skiing on the bunny slope for most of us, drinking lots of hot chocolate, and on a brief detour on the way back to Rantoul, standing at the lectern in the senate of the state capitol building in Madison, Wisconsin. I remember drifting to sleep on the drive home, glancing at Mr. Quint and wondering if he might drift to sleep along with the rest of us. He guided us expertly through winter weather—a snowstorm on icy roads. He cared for each of us, so I think I let go and fell asleep assured that we'd be safe with Mr. Quint at the wheel.

Mr. and Mrs. Quint embraced me and shared the events of their lives with me in written communications and phone calls long after I graduated and moved around the country. Mrs. Quint is a faithful correspondent, but my phone calls and visits always involved conversation with both her and Mr. Quint. Mrs. Quint would answer the phone, but before too long it was a rollicking three-way conversation.

My last visit with them both was in late March of 2007. Mr. Quint was tired and noticeably uncomfortable at times, but his sense of humor was intact, and he entertained Mrs. Quint and me for an hour or so with stories about his daughters and their children. When Mr. Quint spoke about his youngest granddaughter, it was as though a lantern lit him from inside. It's no exaggeration to say that his memories of them entirely transformed his somewhat fatigued and somber demeanor. He adored his family and always made his friends feel at ease and loved.

In the last day or so, Charlie shared some wonderful stories with me about the many friendships Mr. Quint nurtured during his long life. It occurs to me that he knew exactly where the value of life lay—in the relationships we have with our family and our friends. He demonstrated for his many friends, and I feel so privileged to count myself among that honored group, the way to get the most out of life by getting the most from our relationships with others, and by giving all of ourselves to the people we love. God care for you, dear friend, and give us grace as we adapt to a world without your physical presence.

WORDS OF REMEMBRANCE OF RICHARD C. QUINT
JULY 22, 1922–MARCH 25, 2008
by Charlene Quint Kalebic

Thank you for coming today and honoring Dick by being here to remember my dad. We so very much appreciate your presence and friendship and support. The cards and letters and e-mails and phone calls and dinners and flowers and the beautiful DVD that Kelly Vetter made and my college roommate showing up at my door this morning and the flowers from Dad's Angels of Ebermannstadt, halfway around the world, and just seeing everyone here to encourage us—is frankly overwhelming and undeserved. We are humbled and we feel so very, very blessed.

I see so many familiar faces, and I know that you are here because Dick touched your life—and you touched his. Most of you knew my dad as a friend or a neighbor or a colleague. But I would like to share with you a few thoughts about being Dick Quint's daughter.

ADVENTURE

Helen Keller once said "Life is either a daring adventure or nothing." And if you were Dick's daughter, life was one big adventure. His free spirit, love of adventure, and fondness for all things of the Great West was evident in the way that he raised us. When we were young, it often meant that Saturdays were spent at an auction. These excursions weren't always planned, of course; they were more serendipitous. On our way to or from Saturday morning errands, Dad would see a sign for an auction at some far-off farm in the hinterlands, and away we went to explore all the treasures we could find. My sister Kathy scratched her head at one, and we ended up with a pump organ!

Vacations were adventures in themselves, as we all packed up in the back of the station wagon or Suburban with the beloved Airstream trailer behind us and headed out for the open road and whatever might come our way—never with any reservations or a set plan, but just a general direction and a sense of anticipation of what might come. Often the general direction was west to the mountains, where Dad had spent his younger years as a cowboy on a ranch.

Given the average age of our vehicles, I actually don't remember a vacation which did not include a stop for vehicle breakdowns—that was just part of the adventure. And Dad, of course, fixed them all. There was the three-day stay in beautiful Minot, North Dakota, for a broken axle on the trailer (two days waiting for the part to come in and one day replacing the axle), a one-day stay on Christmas Day at the Grand Canyon in ten-below weather for a broken radiator, and numerous breakdowns to and from Florida. We never really minded—we always met the nicest and most interesting people who helped us out during these little detours. So as I got older and went to college in the eighties, the fact that my 1966 Chevy which Dad bought for four hundred dollars with no floorboards was always breaking down did not faze me at all—I would either fix the flat tire or uncooperative carburetor myself, or hitchhike until I could find someone who could. I met some pretty interesting people myself on those trips. I came to appreciate the quote by G.K. Chesterton that, "An adventure is only an inconvenience rightly considered."

When I turned about nine, it became apparent that Dad and I shared the same spirit of exploration, while Mom and Kathy were more homebodies. Thus began the beginning of many of "Dick and Charlie's Excellent Adventures." One of our first excellent adventures together was Dick teaching me to water-ski behind Bud Vetter's boat when I was about ten. After an afternoon of failed attempts, he jumped in the water with all his clothes on and showed me how to do it. When I was about fourteen and he was fifty-five, we decided that we needed to learn to snow ski. Living in the cornfields did not provide many opportunities for that, so off we went to the hills of Wisconsin to take our first of several ski trips. I must admit, seeing my dad on the bunny slopes at age fifty-five was somewhat amusing, but one of the kids came up to me and said, "Gee, I wish my dad would do that with me." I was beginning to learn what a special guy he was.

The next year, he took me and about six of my high school friends on a weekend ski trip. He seemed to love being in the thick of young folks—and they loved him. Even as an adult, when I told him that I had bought a Harley Davidson motorcycle and planned to take motorcycle lessons, he wanted to come along and take them too—and he did, at the tender age of seventy-five.

EUROPE/WORLD WAR II

Our biggest adventure was a life-changing trip for all of us in 2004 when our family retraced Dad's footsteps through Europe at the sixtieth anniversary of the Allied Invasion at Normandy. Dad and I went back again in 2005 to continue the visits that we weren't able to fit in the previous year. By then he was eighty-two, and I thought he was old. I was wrong.

Our journey to Europe was Dad's victory lap at the end of a life well-lived. It is something few of us ever have the opportunity to do. He was able to survey the good work that he had started when he was just seventeen and enlisted in the army and was able to see the fruits of his labor—the rebuilding and success of a *free* Germany and a *free* Belgium and a *free* France. He was able to extend a hand of friendship and forgiveness to eighty-something-year-old German soldiers who came up to him time and time again, trying to explain in broken English that they had no choice but to fight or else be slaughtered along with their families at the hands of the Nazis. They desperately wanted to reach out to an American soldier and explain their plight and receive forgiveness.

He was able to report back to an East German woman that he had kept his promise to her mother and had traveled all the way from Minnesota to Chicago to find her brother and deliver a note she had written. He was able to encourage men and women who, like himself, have made it their personal mission to promote peace and friendship—among nations and between neighbors—beginning with themselves. He was able to say good-bye to and to show a dear friend how much he appreciated her kindness and friendship and that of her family when he was billeted in their home. He was able to give sage words of wisdom as active members of the service asked him for advice as they struggled with survivor's guilt while their friends had fallen in battle. He was able to finally hear the thank-yous and the heartfelt gratitude of the people whose land he helped liberate—the free people of France, and Belgium, and Germany. He was able to hear the thankfulness of the British people and the British soldiers, his brothers-in-arms in a battle in which losing was not an option. He was able to sign autographs and pose for pictures and give interviews and be nothing short of a rock star for a few weeks.

But perhaps most important of all, like a doting and protective big brother, he was able to ensure that the flame of faith and friendship in the hearts and souls of his beloved Angels of Ebermannstadt burned brightly—and he ensured that the torch was passed to the next two generations.

These voyages gave me insight into my dad's character that I had never seen before. I was able to see the people and hear the stories, the stories of faith and kindness in the midst of war, that formed him into the person he was. Our visit gave me a new appreciation of my dad, along with his fellow heroes. I was able to look past the older man's body to see the young man he really was. Our visit was not to see the great sights and sounds of Europe. No, our visit was a mission for him and a well-needed sermon for me in life's greatest lessons. It was a farewell tour in the twilight of his life. Our visit was Dick's last effort to reconnect with people who had been kind to him, to let people know their trust in him had not been not misplaced, to restore relationships, and to let the people he held dear in his life know that he cherished them.

First, last, and always, Dick treasured relationships—with his heavenly Father and with his fellow man. He lived out, in his own practical, unassuming way, what he had learned in Sunday school—what Jesus said are our greatest commandments—love God, and love your neighbor. Dad was once again teaching me lessons, and I wasn't even aware that I had signed up for class.

ENCOURAGEMENT

In St. Paul's letter to the church at Ephesus, he tells us to encourage one another and to say only things that will be a blessing to each other. One of the nicest things about being Dick's daughter is that we knew we always had a fan club. No matter what harebrained idea we came up with, he was 100 percent behind us. When I was seven, he helped coach my little league baseball team. When I was in junior high, he fully supported my efforts to have a car wash to support the little-known Albert Schweitzer Foundation in Africa. When I was sixteen, he put me on a plane to Brazil to be a foreign exchange student—and in return he put up with a foreign exchange student in our house for months, playing tour guide throughout the entire Midwest. He carted Kathy and me around to every form of lesson we could think of: piano lessons, horseback riding lessons, ice skating lessons, even baton twirling lessons. And he sat through countless baseball games and choir concerts and track meets and musicals and anything else that we could get ourselves involved in.

In college, in the days before instant messaging and e-mails, he took the time to clip out words from magazines and paste them into letters and posters—just so he could mail us something different from a plain handwritten letter. There was seldom a week when I didn't get a custom-made letter from Dad along with some homemade cookies from Mom. And he frequently just showed up on campus—which was great because it meant that he took me and all my friends out to dinner and the local ice cream parlor instead of suffering through more cafeteria food. As an adult, there was no better person for fixing up houses, hauling furniture, or supporting our choice of careers and families.

Dick excelled at grandparenthood and brought to it the same enthusiasm he did to parenthood. Whether it was bringing a new baby home from the hospital, introducing a child to a herd of buffalo, teaching him the fine art of shooting a gun, or going on camping adventures, the grandkids always knew they had a friend in Grandpa.

HOSPITALITY

In St. Paul's letter to the Romans, he tells us to "practice hospitality"—not just once in a while, but to make it a habit. And the book of Hebrews tells us to "Entertain strangers, for in doing so, you have entertained angels unaware." Growing up as Dick's daughter, you knew you would have guests for dinner nearly every Sunday. He taught machine shop, metals, and nondestructive testing at Chanute Air Force Base for years, and the U.S. military and our allies would send their troops to Chanute for school from all over the world. He had a big heart for foreigners in a foreign land, whether they were from Ethiopia or Minnesota. And Chanute being a foreign land, he figured the best way to make them feel at home was to have them over for Sunday pot roast—comfort food. I know Dick was thinking of the students in his class, "His family is halfway across the world and its Thanksgiving. Let's have him over." It was like the United Nations at our house, and we loved it. We learned Spanish from the Columbians, Swahili from the Kenyans, and even Minnesotan from the Minnesotans. Yeah—hey der! Uff dah!

FRIENDSHIPS

A Nigerian proverb says, "Hold a true friend with both hands." I don't have to tell you that my dad loved people—that is why you all are here. He loved you! He loved all different kinds of folks—you didn't have to look like him or be like him or act like him or even be anywhere close to his age for him to like you. He liked all sorts of folks. For him, a stranger was just a friend he hadn't met yet. I never heard him say an unkind thing about anybody. And one of the greatest things about being Dick Quint's daughter is that he had some fantastic friends—a group from the air force base, the boys club at McDonald's, folks around town. There were a bunch of really colorful characters who made our lives all the more interesting.

When I was a kid, Bud Vetter, of course, seemed bigger than life—now *he* was a character. He always told you exactly what he was thinking—no filtration allowed. His wife, Doris, was one of the most delightful people I have ever known, and it was always a treat to be able to hang out with her. And, of course, if my dad was friends with you, he was friends with every generation. This means that he has enjoyed friendships with four generations of Vetters—and I have to tell you, he thought the world of each of you.

All of you sitting here were part of the wonderful fabric of our lives and Dick's life—and we are clearly the richer for it.

As teenagers, there was no doubt that if you were a friend of ours, you were automatically a friend of Dick's. And if you were a friend of Dick's, then your parents were his friends too. This definitely had some upsides. Because my dad was so fond of our friends and their parents, he trusted us—maybe a little too much. Strangely enough, while I did have a curfew most of the time, if I was with my group of friends who knew Dad, curfew didn't apply. He knew I was in good hands. There were some downsides to this, of course, in that we couldn't get into too much trouble because our parents would compare notes and talk to each other. But even now, into adulthood, our childhood friends and their parents continue their friendship with us.

Mentoring/Teaching

The book of 1 Corinthians tells us that one of God's gifts is teaching. And as a daughter of Dick Quint, one of the things that runs through my veins is teaching. Both Jean and Dick were teachers. And anyone who knew my dad knew that not only did he love to teach, he loved to mentor young people. He knew the importance of having a loving father in one's life—because he never had one. He left home at thirteen to become a cowboy. He had a soft spot in his heart for young men who might not have had the ideal upbringing or a loving father figure in their lives. One of his greatest joys was coming along beside them, teaching and mentoring and encouraging them, and being the one thing that everyone needs: someone who believes in them. He loved watching them become successful young men and husbands and fathers. And if Dick Quint came and walked along beside you, you knew that it wasn't for a summer or a season or even a year. He invested in you for his entire life. You know who you are—Dick really loved each one of you.

Some of these young men, now in their sixties, have called me over the last several days and weeks, often with tears in their eyes, to share some wonderful stories. "Your dad was more of a dad to me than my dad," is a recurring theme. I thought my sister and I were the only ones to lose a dad, but I now realize that we are joined by others for whom Dick filled the empty shoes of "Dad."

Music

Psalm 100 says "Sing a joyful song to the Lord." Being Dick's daughter meant that you had a lot of music in your life. Dick was a whistler; we always knew where he was by his whistle. And there is something about whistlers—they are happy, optimistic people. And there is just something about being happy and optimistic that makes you want to be around them. He also loved to sing and was a barbershopper for some time. I remember as a little girl sitting on his lap while he sang to me, "If You Were the Only Girl in the World" and "I'm Forever Blowing Bubbles" and "Lida Rose," and of course the old hymns and cowboy songs. He passed his love of music down to us—and after he and Mom suffered through violin lessons and flute lessons where we sounded more like sick geese than musicians, we finally landed on a love of the piano that has lasted a lifetime and has passed to Dick and Jean's grandchildren as well.

SELF-RELIANCE

Being a Quint girl also meant that you knew how to use power tools, change a tire, ride a horse, shoot a shotgun, and check your own darn oil. You knew every tool in the toolbox and how to use it, and how to drive a stick shift. It also meant that you were not afraid of spiders, mice, rats, snakes, or any other critter that might come along. Unpaid summer projects could include anything from painting the house to building a brick patio. There were no sissies allowed.

GOOD WORKS

The book of James tell us that the kind of religion God approves is doing good works and looking after orphans and widows. Part of being raised a Quint meant that when we had no idea where Dad was, there was a good bet that he was helping someone out. Whether it was fixing a screen door, shoveling snow, mowing a lawn, fixing tractors and cars, reading stories to children at the children's home, more recently collecting and sending care packages full of toys to Iraqi children, or—I think his personal favorite—trying to find that elusive whatchamacallit for someone at some auction or flea market, he was *always* helping someone. That was just part of his makeup.

I recall coming home from college once only to find our wonderful childhood tree house missing from the backyard. Dad had built it out of telephone poles and lumber with a tin roof and a rope ladder, and Kathy and I had spent many happy summer childhood afternoons up there. He had disassembled it and given it to our neighbor across the street who was a single mom with a little boy, and then, of course, reassembled it in their backyard—*my* tree house! I should have known—that was just how he was. This little boy needed a tree house, and he was going to give him one. He wanted to help others, not because of a sense of obligation, but because he genuinely loved to do so.

THANKFULNESS

Dad's favorite quote was by Helen Keller: "So much has been given to me, I have no time to ponder over that which has been denied." One of the things about being a Quint meant that we knew Dad was thankful for every blessing he had. He looked at everything in his life—his wife, his family, his friends, his job, his home, everything—like it was a treasured gift, not as an entitlement. And as I have gotten older, I have realized that having that "attitude of gratitude" does two marvelous things: first, it keeps you humble when you realize that literally everything in your life is a gift from above. And second, it keeps you happy, because you are so busy being thankful you don't have time to complain. And Dad was both humble and happy because he was so grateful. His happiness overflowed into a wonderful sense of humor. You could expect a good belly laugh at least once a day if you were with him.

Even in his last days, when it would be understandable if he were to complain, he had a thankful heart. The very last day we all saw him, he could barely speak it was such an effort. But he told us that he was so appreciative that we visited so much; he told us how great it was to have a big family. When I mentioned that I had spoken to his doctor that day, he said "She is such a delightful person." And of course, he told us he loved us.

JEAN

Father Theodore Hesburgh, one of the great religious leaders of our time, said, "The best thing a father can do for his children is love their mother." There was no doubt that my mother, Jean, was the love of his life. He would always tell us what a treasure she was to him, and he would often praise her in front of others. "That girl right there," he would say, "I am so lucky to have her." In his last few months, I would visit him nearly every day, and I decided that I needed to know his top ten secrets to a lifelong happy marriage to pass down to his grandchildren. We only got through the top three before he had a stroke and couldn't continue—but they were probably the only three anyone needs to know anyway. The first: don't marry the devil's grandmother. (I think this was some reference to a prior relationship, but I didn't go there.) The second: marry someone like your mother. The third: understand each other. And I think that pretty much covers the important stuff.

FAITH

One of the greatest gifts our dad ever gave us was the gift of faith. He had a personal relationship with Jesus that started when he was a young boy, and they walked together throughout his entire life. And he imparted the importance of a personal friendship with Jesus to us. When someone asked Jesus what the most important rules in the Bible were, Jesus didn't come out with a long list of rules. He said only two things: love God with all your mind and soul and heart and strength, and love your neighbor as yourself. For Him, it was all about your relationship with God and your relationship with others. And I think Dad tried to live out just that.

If you are at all interested in knowing about the kind of faith my dad had, I invite you to seek me out after the service. I would love to talk to you about it. He wasn't a saint, oh no. He just knew that he was imperfect and full of faults—and that he needed God in his life, as we all do. If you knew him, you knew that he didn't preach or evangelize; I don't remember getting any lectures about how we should be living our lives. But in his own quiet way, he went about doing the Lord's work here on earth of encouraging others, helping others, being a father to the fatherless, being a loving husband, and being the best dad I could ever ask for.

No, our dad did not tell us how to live. He lived life the way it should be lived—and he let us watch him do it.

BAND OF BROTHERS

If we are mark'd to die, we are enow
To do our country loss; and if to live,
The fewer men, the greater share of honour.
God's will! I pray thee, wish not one man more.

By Jove, I am not covetous for gold,
Nor care I who doth feed upon my cost;
It yearns me not if men my garments wear;
Such outward things dwell not in my desires.

But if it be a sin to covet honour,
I am the most offending soul alive.
No, faith, my coz, wish not a man from England.
God's peace! I would not lose so great an honour
As one man more methinks would share from me
For the best hope I have. O, do not wish one more!

Rather proclaim it, Westmoreland, through my host,
That he which hath no stomach to this fight,
Let him depart; his passport shall be made,
And crowns for convoy put into his purse;
We would not die in that man's company
That fears his fellowship to die with us.

This day is call'd the feast of Crispian.
He that outlives this day, and comes safe home,
Will stand a tip-toe when this day is nam'd,
And rouse him at the name of Crispian.

He that shall live this day, and see old age,
Will yearly on the vigil feast his neighbours,
And say 'To-morrow is Saint Crispian.'
Then will he strip his sleeve and show his scars,
And say 'These wounds I had on Crispian's day.'

Old men forget; yet all shall be forgot,
But he'll remember, with advantages,
What feats he did that day. Then shall our names,
Familiar in his mouth as household words—
Harry the King, Bedford and Exeter,
Warwick and Talbot, Salisbury and Gloucester-
Be in their flowing cups freshly remember'd.

This story shall the good man teach his son;
And Crispin Crispian shall ne'er go by,
From this day to the ending of the world,
But we in it shall be remembered—

We few, we happy few, we band of brothers;
For he to-day that sheds his blood with me
Shall be my brother; be he ne'er so vile,
This day shall gentle his condition;

And gentlemen in England now-a-bed
Shall think themselves accurs'd they were not here,
And hold their manhoods cheap whiles any speaks
That fought with us upon Saint Crispin's day.

—ST. CRISPIN'S DAY SPEECH OF 1415
WILLIAM SHAKESPEARE, HENRY V (1599)

AUTHOR'S NOTE

If *Angels of Ebermannstadt* has been a blessing to you, please share how it has blessed you. Likewise, if you would like to share your own inspirational story of faith, friendship, and light shining in the darkness, I would love to hear from you. If you would like your story to be considered for an upcoming inspirational book, please include your contact information.

Mail or emails received may be shared on our website guestbook.

Please contact me at:

Charlene Quint Kalebic

Inspiration Breaks

P.O. Box 230

230 Northgate

Lake Forest, IL 60045

Phone: 847-505-8069

E-mail: charlene@charlenequintkalebic.com

Website: www.CharleneQuintKalebic.com